Questology

The Logic in Quest

within

the compass of the mind

by
Thomas Vato

Copyright © 2018 by Thomas Vato

ISBN-13: 978-1726442688

ISBN-10: 1726442683

All rights reserved. No parts of this publication may be reproduced, scanned, or transmitted in any form, digital or printed, without the written permission of the author.

Contents

Preface

Chapter 1:
The first step into questology   1

Chapter 2:
Practical fundamentals of progress: DPL
1. The Decisions   15
2. The Problems   37
3. The Leadership of the Question   51

Chapter 3:
The First Principle of Questology -
The Question-Answer Bridge   61

Chapter 4:
Translating present to the future
By putting future into present   75

Chapter 5:
The Second Principle of Questology -
The Mental Architecture   99
To upgrade a brilliant culture
- The Law of Acuity   114
- The Law of Division   132
- The Law of Refinement   138

Chapter 6:
The Third Principle of Questology -
The Logic in Quest   160
- Triadic style - The Function and Ability   167
- Askability score - The Fitness and Utility   200

Chapter 7:
The Fourth Principle of Questology -
Complexity Management   222
- The Complex Fabric of Understanding   231
- Learning as Electricity of Progress   252
- Mental Property Taxes & The Cognitive Entanglement   277
- The Step of Detachment   307

• Going Light   330

The Ending Note

Preface

Questology is to liberate from the self-imposed limitation and think for yourself. The book stands for individualism, freedom, and intellect. The question is the leader to change and improve the age. To make seeing today's things differently than yesterday's and tomorrow's unlike today's. To avoid falling into a rut, but create the way you will trust. To envision the time to come with all the possibilities it could become. In this book, the question brings the answer to make the mind a prolific dancer. Answers you need to succeed.

No matter the definition of success - every mind can cover up in the finest dress. What is more important than this is progress. It is natural that people want to know things. You may wish to excellent health, more wealth or improvement in yourself. It implies partial incompletion. To fulfil a thing means knowing answers how to get to places where the relevant answer is. Then the question becomes the agent to push your mind into engagement. There, you will discover a method of thinking to guide yourself with questions.

To solve problems, make decisions and build progress - thinking is the king. Advice for thinking may be hazy - perhaps the claim for righteousness and being lazy. To think is great, but the output may be showing little ink. To write the novelty on the current plate is never late. The thought is pensive while questioning becomes more practical and active. That is where the change transpires, and the mind becomes one of the unpreventable suppliers. To supply the question to get your response - employ thinking to satisfy your needs and wants. Just ask - this is the flair to pose a question in the air. The compass which navigates your mind with the logic in quest.

Why do you need questology? Look at the evolution of history posing us a delightful symphony. The world has witnessed Renaissance of Culture - in the Mondial history it is a shining sculpture. The Age of Exploration did cause a mighty transformation. Equally, the Century of Lights has built the bridge for Human Rights. Then, the Industrial Revolution has been bringing a positive solution. And in the Age of Wars many empires have lost their scores. Eventually, in times of information and technology here comes questology - the champion of logic, inquisitiveness and expansive thinking.

A target of the profession in this book is not a fundamental question. Today, the air of innovation and constructive thinking become a new progressive thing. No matter if you are pensive, active or creative - questology is a good incentive. You might be a leader, whose thoughts and actions will inspire your reader; or a bold entrepreneur making complicated things clear; why not a writer who wishes to transform your verbal skills into something lighter? For you as an executive who wants to be the most competitive. If you are a designer, it will assist you to make your craft finer. Also, for the creative or a thinker to stop living in the winter, and for a scientist to discover what do not exist. For a member of society who might have been living quietly. The name of questologist - a novel walk of life which has started to exist.

In the end, questology is the mental structure to replace a stagnant culture. Questology wants to dispel prejudice to produce enjoyment and pleasant smell. For the expression of an idea, people are not risking as in North Korea. It is better to ask questions because free speech more than violence in streets will teach. Sometimes we seek for various answers as if we were exhausted dancers. Things you want to know may have been done some years ago. To get fresh and vigorous remind yourself your questions because uncertain steps into any new arena may feel like dancing as an obese ballerina. With questions it is temporary.

It is the tool to discover logic to use it for its practical benefits. In exploration, discoveries, and inventions, questions are practical. Significant developments and designs were made having deep curiosity and interest behind. Devices like the light bulb, the computer or the airplane - are not those practically valuable? Those are inventions. To invent things questions contribute significantly. Admittedly, there is plenty of work done in between a question and the answer. The question of how to create something - the answer is the invention. The more inventive you become, the more progress the world can experience. This book wants this.

Everyone can do more than that. Exploration and discoveries are to refresh entrenched patterns. If you assume a productive model which requires input x to get output y, then it pushes someone into a repetitive and habitual existence. Nobody will rebuke for the effectiveness of current things someone does. Repetition is often the requirement for any achievement. This book employs questions in the position to improve patterns of things in use. It designs the compass to navigate in any new arena no matter how you define what is unfamiliar. Questions translate unfamiliar into familiar where common was unknown at first. Also, they escape from patterns to bring novelty, refresh understanding and to reinvent things. Discoveries support the effort both practical and intellectual.

Then, to question is to think sounds like a premise. This book connects thinking with questioning under one flag. The generalisation telling that silence in a grave mimic means thinking is deceptive. Even the fool can look thoughtful. Intelligent and smart looking is just cosmetics in appearance. This book neglects looks and focuses more on actions, performance, and achievements with a hidden beauty beneath. Questions are the beginner to achieve needed answers and become a winner. They expose thinking to end up with answers. Knowledge is the result of the answered question. So being able to extract productive learning starts from questions. To question is to think - almost equivalent. What you need is to think before getting what you want.

However, that is not all. This book goes for the unconventional leadership. The question delegates the mind which is the leader to drive your mind to your finely selected direction. No matter what dimension you may choose to guide yourself. It may be personal, social, professional or whatever field for a positive initiative. Questions are there to escape from the repetitive pattern to start something new, fresh and productive. The leadership of the question is leading your mind while your mind governs this leader.

The act of asking questions navigate the mind. Such is the bizarre statement of leadership. Before someone is considered to be a good leader, questions are the first start. You may agree that leaders are those who have the flair to pose the question in the air to direct attention and skills. The brilliant mind is a better leader than a person who looks brilliant. Questions are to claim leadership because they lead your thoughts. Before command of anything, one often becomes an excellent self-commander. Questology then is about to be the compass of the mind. The tool to design questions to activate oneself towards a specific direction. Ability to lead yourself with mental agility is a good sign of purpose and direction.

Besides, decision making and problem solving are the inevitable spice of life. As you know, the life is imperfect, so there would be something to improve by making decisions. Alternatively, something to enhance by dealing with problems. Problem solving and decision making are universal. It is rare or almost impossible to avoid them. You make hundreds of decisions every day by default. Decisions and choices set in motion your behaviour and the way of thinking. Decision making is the curse - you cannot avoid them. If someone decided to outmanoeuvre them, one has already fixed up its focus. What a decision!

Another universal thing is a problem. If someone says that there is no problem, so one is either does not see or ignore them. Issues are everywhere. Some are extreme and urgent while others appear in a slight form of inconvenience. Having the fridge empty, a house on fire or underperforming finances - all of them express minor troubles in their shades of uniqueness. Problems have many shades. It starts with inconvenience that there is no milk for tea or coffee to tragedies where bombers destroy entire cities in war zones. There, intensity shapes problem's identity. Then, the solution is the answer where the question ends up in conclusion.

Moving forward, to think is to compute. Computers are considered to be excellent thinkers because they run on precise algorithms - to give an analogy. Similarity quickly comes in. Thinking is an act of logic where rules apply to extract conclusions from data. Algorithms are to solve problems. What unites computer and a person is logic. A person uses logic for thinking. Logic is metallic, so as grammar is. Like a foundation for the question to stand on. Then questions stand up on logic to solve problems with the logic in quest.

There are probably no cases where there would be impossible to pose questions. Is it...? Humans question, humans think, and they compute so produce questions to reach answers they need. The mindset is like an individual program having its logic - a personal one. The set of rules governs actions. Actions are visible where reasonable rules stay behind - concealed, but sensible. Someone will say if things make sense or not according to the thinking framework in use. Thinking patterns have logic inside.

Questions have their structure which acts stably. This book is to display the invisible to tackle the visible.

Eventually, both the computer and the mindset runs on logic. The reason why anyone shall care at any degree it is because your mind with the logic in quest will solve problems similarly. The problem is inevitable. Nobody is protected from even the slightest degree of inconvenience and discomfort. What is not very smooth becomes problematic in the most abstract sense. There is you to solve it. You use logic as well as the computer does. A computer cannot question things where you have the advantage. So the advancement goes led by the logic in quest. None of the relevant problems are left unquestioned until the answer comes for dinner. Relevant answers are useful, and questions are leading there.

The question is the answer. What you need is the answer, how to get there is a good question. Issues of science, technology, economy or whatever you pick - the spectre is broad. With the logic in quest, impossible starts looking difficult. Difficulty declines where impossible eventually becomes done. Crippling problems get solved if you start with honest questions. Questology brings a slight hostility in its DNA where curiosity and ability question things with agility. It strives for innovation and betterment in general. The question is the change in itself. Do not let your focus to be misled, because questology appeals only to your head.

In fact, running the mind on questions will result in some way of enlightenment. There is not the moment of fear because questology delivers you only clean air. The sea of everyday complexity is the noise to remove to improve. To establish the straightest line possible between questions and answers is to institute the first principle of questology. To accomplish something meaningful, a smart way is to go straight to the goal. As the conventional compass shows the North, questology points out at the answer - something you need and want. The first principle says that question sets up a direction, while response finishes it. That is the line. This public knowledge may boost hopeful aspirations. Every problem has the answer. The answer you need individually.

Questology itself is more than open questions. Everyone will find out lists of questions which often are quite useful to learn. In this context, there is logic behind all questions. This logic stands on the mental architecture which tends to govern things you think about - the second principle of questology. The reason why we include the mental architecture which you will discover soon is that even if you know how to ask a question, you shall know how to behave with answers. Relevant questions sometimes become inaccessible because questology gives the power to produce questions unlimitedly what puts the mind in the noise. You decide relevance by other means. You come up with the mental architecture - the government behind questions.

The mental architecture is steady to make your mind ready. Further development goes for the logic in quest to fulfil the compass of the mind. The structural aspect of mind starts becoming elastic in the end. Many will recognise logic. It requires more effort to apply existing knowledge to derive new knowledge. Discoveries and inventions shall expand existing conventions. The logic in quest embodies the method and spontaneity. The logic in quest pushes the mind to unlock problems as if it was opening a closed chest.

Asking question shall be the style of mind. Questions energise you and lead the mind outside the zone of comfortable thinking sooner or later. There is more than one way of looking at things. For solving problems and making decisions, the advantageous position is to see more than from one side. The fourth and the last principle of questology goes for complexity management. The wording goes for itself - the world is complicated. The diversity of everything including opinions, theories, and information in general make the world complex where you act in it. Complexity is a common problem in the Information Age what may put a barrier between you and the future. The principle liberates the mind and designs the future. You will find many ways to get there. None of them is right - only those leading there. Future does not exist yet, so neither it can be right.

The flair to pose the question in the air is the natural expression of optimism towards the future. Questions find answers there. Any need of the answer implies the future. Questions target solutions for problems and decisions for current dilemmas. There is the apparent relationship between the present and the future. Questology brings a methodic approach, rational design, model and the mindset with a specific purpose on its target. It brings to the fundamental point that anything someone looks the answer to, the answer is in the future. Because otherwise, questions would be already answered, so there would be no need to find them out. You want now, and you get it later.

Questology

Chapter 1:
The first step into questology

"Like snails, we were fixed to our shells, and I declare it is easy to lead a snail's life."
Jules Verne

A well known Latin phrase "sapere aude" means dare to know. It was the manifest of the age of reason which had reached its peak around 250 years ago. Nowadays, we adopt the phrase and translate it to the new heights. We transit from daring to know to dare to question what means almost the same thing. The question is the force pushing knowledge and understanding forward. Why may someone possibly be against anything better compared to now? Once claimed for liberation and bravery to think, now, the phrase restores its meaning where questioning goes for betterment.

In the metaphoric terms, questology is the compass of the mind. The mental model to see what is given to direct the energy where it is driven. It aims to make questioning into a mental style where an individual dares to be original. Designing own progress and taking from the future everything, but nothing less. Thinking is useful and impractical, but questioning makes it practical. Through questions, you expose your thinking to move forward. The idea translates into questions where the abstract becomes more convenient. So then questions open up the gates for implementing your mind.

A question is a powerful weapon against complexity everybody faces daily. The delicate point is that entanglement interrupting our daily life does not ask for any permission. Evolution advances the initial simplicity into complexity pushed by information, science, technology, social norms or whatever - things tend to increase in their complications. Complexity perplexes the mind unless the mind manages complexity. Questions have their clarifying effect. Otherwise, there is enough noise to sink in the sea of complexity. The question is the way out.

There are at least two options towards complexity. First, to surrender the influence of environment or, second, to apply your mind to get back the control out of complexity. Either you lead complexity, or it leads you. Basic economics tell if you want something, you shall give something by trading your time, energy, skills, resources, or capital. There is a tiny chance that someone will give you something for nothing. Trade is the way to get the thing you want. Entitlement does not work there. Passivity does not bring you any benefit, so you shall take your approach and edit it. Questioning is the method to find out how. Questions trade time, energy and skills to answers which govern complexity.

The active approach is much more productive, is not it? Actions of any kind bring earning consequences. There, questology steps to vote for activity. Questology is the new arena - a vaguely heard term, something designed. The logic in quest for active and curious mind where questions claim for leadership. Logic and intentional questions are the natural sources for questology. It augments untangling ability and decisive agility, so problems get solved, and decisions are made. Those are intended.

As the compass of the mind, questology is not only a mental thing. It starts with thinking patterns and continues in practice. Thoughtful conclusions outgrow into actions where mental becomes practical. Questology is mostly related to the mind and designed to exercise. The good thing is that questions connect with answers like reasons combine with consequences or actions join results. Causality is a principle or the law working regardless of somebody wants it or not.

So the compass of the mind exercises for the guidance. The metaphor is for starting ideas and actions with questions. Questology covers any area imaginable because any set of actions, situations, knowledge, and understanding are questionable with the logic in quest. Principles to create questions contrast with lists of questions. The method to question is superior to records. Lists of specific issues are useful in any industry, but ability to challenge plays a part for independent reasoning. Independence for the mind is a desirable accomplishment.

Then, questioning, like any skill, has a precise structure which is invisible, inaudible and untouchable. This is one among the reasons why questology may look unattainable in the first place. However, like any skill, it exposes itself in use. Mastering the flair to pose a question in the air brings the power to bake questions. The talent is invisible before action. Swimming skill is hidden as well. Only when a person swims you see the skill. The logic in quest is a skill - invisible itself because it is the function. But like swimming - obvious. When the person asks productive questions, ability manifests itself. No matter the goal, questions lead to answers depending on each preference.

As questology appears to be the compass - where are the arrows pointing out? The conventional compass will open up understanding of the North, South, West, and East. What happens to questology then? Such compass has four principles enabling the entire function. The function which equates to the mind. Instead of mind, it would be the compass. Like an intelligent function - the logic in quest. Questology is the more significant expansion of logic. In this context, logic combines with your intentions. Either you have needs or wants - they are targeted to be accomplished. With the logic in quest.

Moreover, the mental compass, as well as the conventional one, is perfect for exploration and discovery. After all, it is the question which guides the ship. Metaphorically, a person is like a ship, and it goes towards where the arrow guides it. The life is like the journey, and you hold the compass. Either you use it and go through, or the life consumes you for itself. The mind is what leads you with questions or without. A given pattern will bring you the option to use your life. Questions can open up multiple ways to guide yourself. Questology liberates from servitude to the given limits. The limit separates your intention from the answer. The answer is what is out of current limits because otherwise, you would hold it already. The compass of the mind is to navigate in complexity.

History is often an excellent source to provide inspiring examples to picture the case. Assume a historical figure - a traveler of 13th century Italy. He was Marco Polo who famed for his journey to China. Being European he opened environment to new ideas of which he returned to Europe. This connects with the central benefits exploration may bring to improve conditions. In this context, an idea of paper money, complex post system, and gunpowder flowed as an indirect result of the Marco Polo's journey. Just because he went to China and found out something that did not exist in Europe.

However, it does not seem remarkable looking from the current standpoint though. In contrast, now, cashless money, telecommunication networks or atomic weapons are comprehensively more advanced than that. What Marco Polo did was new and progressive for the 13th century, but looks primitive for the 21st one. He was among the first Europeans to visit China for specific missions.

You may imagine the massive step outside the comforting environment. You realise that trains, airplanes or cars did not exist in the 13th century what makes the whole matter more complicated. Such travels will equate for exploration and adventure. It brings the climate of uncertainty and the condition to manage with navigation. The safe environment has its benefits, but is always incomplete because beyond boundaries there are more things to discover.

Marco Polo is a particular case to represent exploration. The compass and the guide have led through it. His efforts brought valuable things in the end what enriched his first environment. When it comes to the zone of uncertainty, questology is the compass to lead through the smoke of doubt. It does not bring certainty, but the sense of direction to prevent someone from getting lost. There, questions connect with answers like the compass points to the North. Questions are the leaders.

Moving forward, if Marco Polo is not enough for the historical figure, take another one. Another Italian with a famous name - someone who discovered America - Cristopher Columbus. A brave one supported by the Spanish to find the way to India. He did not make what he intended because he hit America. Perhaps considered to be a failure of the time because the primary intent was India. Such discovery is not a disappointing failure though. It instituted a separation between old and new worlds, opened the land of opportunity to trade as well as discovered new agricultural goods, different customs, and new cultures. There was nothing but water - the compass was the device to sail with confidence. The compass is what brings the level of stability in the sea of everyday complexity. Talking about questology, it backs itself upon solid principles founded on logic. Logic is structural, so it does not get affected even by the most terrible storms of life.

Two historical examples already emphasised the guiding force to move forward. Let's be clear, Christoper Columbus did not expect to find America. He was more interested in India for lucrative spice. This outcome was not intended. Moreover, Marco Polo did not expect to discover gunpowder, paper money or complex post system. The seek for fortune eventually led there. Discoveries come unexpectedly for those who explore. The question initiates exploration - every question is a smart start reaching something off the chart.

Questology is indeed a compass to expedite the connection of two distant points in space and time. Either it was a land connection between Italy and China in the 13th century. Or it was a sea connection between Europe and America in the 15th century. As you will discover in the first principle of questology - the question always connects with the answer. Looking for connections, one does not need to ask for directions. Two points on the land, you will understand. Connected across the sea you cannot but agree. Or two points in space will illustrate the upcoming case. The landing on the Moon just after the month after June. This is the past you can remember fast. The important thing is the future where your mind uses logic as a computer.

The final note there goes on importance. What is vital is questology's shape and function of a compass. The logic in quest is what builds up questions around the gravity. Focus, self-composure, and direction are qualities of a bright and committed mind. Many things will not work in achieving something remarkable. Questions will lead you there anyway as long as you keep asking and implementing them.

Everybody wants to know. Everyone requests for a different set of knowledge what makes it supremely important. Someone may think that being productive and successful is far more critical. Knowing what is essential, is a part of reaching success. Knowing how to achieve wealth and prosperity is another part towards. Also, knowing how to govern wealth is superior to just being wealthy. It is all about knowledge.

Exploration, discoveries, inventions, and improvements are excellent examples of progress. Things bring freshness, novelty, and utility - something that uplift societies. Economic growth, increase in happiness metrics or living standards matter significantly. They are particular elements of progress in the most abstract sense. With the compass of the mind, any finely selected area is open for a progression. The most crucial moment is to focus on the type of progress you have a passion for being involved in. The question is the guiding gesture.

No matter what are the metrics of progress - it is measurable. Standards may differ, but progress remains. Playing football has clear rules of the game. Winners score the most. Goals are the score. Capitalism is a similar game to maintain the society moving. The score in the bank account allows to progress needs of the individual and the society. The number in the bank account is to show how well the game is played. No matter which game is to be played. Knowledge of how to play the game successfully without losing contentment is superior to the score.

No matter the standard and metrics to be chosen, progress is improving the numbers and conditions of the current situation.

Getting to the answer improve the score of any game. There are different platforms where people improve with questions. What is more important than the platform took, there are three elements to be always found in them. In this book, they are called practical fundamentals of progress where decisions, problems and the leadership of the question get the attention. Elements which fulfil any field of activity to improve existing conditions and push the limits of excellence.

Chapter 2: Practical fundamentals of progress:

DPL
The Decisions

> *"Management is doing things right, Leadership is doing a right thing."*
> ***Peter Drucker***

Decisions are universal - you cannot escape from them. And so you need to decide on things. Better decisions win preferences over terrible ones. A temptation to avoid decisions lead to consequences of which you may not like. Indecisiveness may bring you into a passive mode. In this case, an actual speed reducer. Progress requires movement, so if the speed is bleak, there is little progress for us to speak. You may have your reason for improvement. Let's say better health, more wealth or stimulation for yourself. If things do not move, they do not change much. So if decisions are not taken, desired consequences do not come. Progress slows down. That is an issue.

The universality of decisions is the practical fundamental of progress. You may hide from decisions, run away or exercise any other evasive way. However, you cannot eliminate choices from the equation of reality. Decisions and their making are in it. If you wanted to remove this from the framework - it is a decision - so it would not work without a contradiction. To not make decisions decisively would be a striking statement. Living your life or flowing apathetically are two choices among others. There is no way to give up your power to decide or choose. To give up your decision power is the decision after all.

To make excellent choices or poor ones improves the skill with every attempt. Someone may think this is too obvious. Fundamental things are elegantly simple, but barely seen due to the veil of complexity which often covers the matter. Unless you get shown in one way or another. You cannot escape decisions, but what you can do is to improve their making quality. Small choices lead to achievement. It does not matter what sort of success you hold in your head. What matters is the awareness of the universality of decisions to get you there. It releases the will to operate them. Hopefully, knowing that is impossible to hide or escape from judgements brings the will to face the music.

Surely, decisions and choices are for consequences. Unsurprisingly common. Secondly, thinking also has its conclusions - another realm. For the third one, questions have their answers. Three examples have a similar line of connection. This is what matters in practice. Decisions are the masterpiece of practicality -

made to bring more self or public interest. Otherwise, there is no point in making them if they do not provide anything valuable. Having nothing to achieve someone may mistreat the importance. The distribution of importance allows people to refrain from unimportant decisions. There are plenty of ways to use available time, energy and attention.

For one thing, this chapter will not be a warehouse to store the most effective ways to make decisions. There are much of advice outside this book where your taste will meet a fitting method for the increased effectiveness. What is more important than lists of methods is the establishment of awareness that there is no escape but choice. Flight is also the choice for failing to win the race. When you have no choice but to choose, more likely you pick what is better than a similar alternative. Most likely, this is the way you choose between partners, products, places to eat and everything around. Decisions are everywhere.

Decisions are the practical fundamental of progress. They bring consequences which are nothing but results. When you consider a starting point, results come from decisions made before. So holding such perspective shall widen up your vision. For the consequence intended, individual choices are needed to be made. It is obvious. Better results are more desired than worse ones. Then decisions are to be made accordingly. For example, better health is better than worse. Fortune is better than poverty. Excitement is better than boredom. People naturally decide on their liking even without telling. Having a broader perspective adds up an advantage.

There are better metrics than despair to make decisions around. Health, wealth or stimulation of yourself - just three for a starter. Many others remain tacitly omitted. Standards are constructions of values. Some people may prefer suffering - that is another metric. Those people may deliberately make choices around that. Admittedly, it would be clever to question either this thing is a satisfying standard. Generally, decisions gravitate around standards while rules fulfil to sustain themselves what makes a loop. Questions are to match or challenge standards to better them up if they have any hint of a defect.

In decisions, you will find the standard to focus on. Background of the decision maker has an impact. Eventually, decisions comply with standards. They decide on things to be agreed upon. Someone's background influences the importance of elements that form the standard. People have different standards as well as they have different experiences and perceptions. The relativity quickly steps in. When you take someone culturally sensitive, and someone who is not, you will see a difference between such couple. For example, archeological elements for one will look like surprising cultural heritage with a spectacular history behind. For someone else, it may seem like plain rocks and stuff. Standards guide perceptions and judgements. People do not have this in the same way. Background and formation play their roles.

The standard in decision making is what aligns complexity of the world into an elegant formula. When people develop their standards, it is straightforward to determine what fits it and what does not. The pattern which includes and excludes something to put extra attention on. For a convenient example, when you are looking for something to buy on Amazon, there are metrics to guide you. It is the price, reviews or any other parameter - different standards to apply for something you search for before making a final decision. If the price or reviews are the metrics, you focus on this, so exclude everything that goes outside the standard. It breaks down the abundance of options til eventually you buy something. The choice is made.

While making decisions, standards serve for focusing attention. There is something to fulfil the standard. Facing any complexity, to make a choice means excluding the unfitting alternatives and dealing with what fits. The standard decides on fitness. If you make a decision, it is already aimed at something. So standard determines what aligns with your aim and what does not. That is a mental design to remove abundant options and extract simplicity. Sounds like a choice according to the standard. The world is too noisy and complicated to pay attention to everything. Standards are the expectations of yours. No matter they are high or low, they filter complexity.

You know that decision making is a process. It is important to realise that making them brings more control over results and consequences. For a rough comparison, when someone makes decisions and acts, consequences come. On the other hand, when no decision is taken, the consequences are out of slightest control. The influence of will on the future is zero. The future has more impact on you than you have on it. Choices are improvable like a skill, and when any dilemma, trilemma or whatemma get executed, the person is more in control over one's outcomes.

Being universal decisions are still diverse. Some choices are light; others demand more time because they remain intricately complicated. Awareness of tough and light ones make someone to choose certain matters better. Questions assist in the decision process. For example, questions bring more information, penetrate the difficulty and improve the skill. Decisions are fundamentals of progress. Habits of thought and action are to reinforce the whole process.

After all, everyday decisions are to receive the art of slight automation. You do not decide on trivial things. You automate choices which make things automatic. Intuitive decision making is advantageous and tricky at the same time. On the one hand, it eliminates mental energy cost. However, on the other hand, automated processes entrenches and will become hard to replace if they start to malfunction.

Decisions are automated or original. Many would agree that repetitive thought demands less mental energy compared to innovative thinking going through new ways. For example, a novice taxi driver will consume a lot of psychological energy making choices to drive a client through the city. Unless one has navigation what tells what to do. Following is less costly compared to inventing the new way. Every new and original decision requires much of mental energy compared to demands of a repetition. It is clear that someone with ten years of experience will demonstrate an exceptional judgement with a lower mental energy cost. Knowledge, in this case, would naturally bring more control over the results because it is automated.

Regarding standards, you will find at least two options to behave with them. Firstly, using questions, someone may be challenging existing rules to spot a flaw and destroy it. The second option is to design your standard based on what exists in the market. This is more constructive than critical. There are many components to design standard to seek for excellence in performance and decision making. So it challenges and crafts standards for a better decision making. Standards guide your decisions.

The first and the foremost standards are not universal - they can be challenged. Decisions are inevitable while standards are more flexible. You can challenge decisions, but you still need to make them in the most abstract sense because you cannot avoid them. Standards are the platform for decisions. When someone has many alternatives, there is the standard to participate in them. Having high standards make decisions significantly easier. What is not good enough to satisfy the rule goes out of frame. Little complexity and abundance get on the scene. However, having low standards bring the abundance which fills it. Then whatemmas of any kind are significantly more difficult because they are plenty. Many things comply with the standard then, so it increases the number of alternatives to consider and make decisions more difficult.

You must realise that you will not find the standard there. What you will see is the compass to design your standards. Standards are the justice in decision making. Every decision will contribute to change. Rules differ in their composition. There are different standards for various fields. The priority there is the authority. For example, in the workplace perhaps being productive is more important than being right. Or, in food probably high quality is much more preferred than other standards - like price and appearance. Coming to backgrounds, values, and preferences - they set up the standard which becomes the filter to make decisions. Finally standard always remains open to question.

Standardisation is the automation of individual decisions. Ever thought to build standards? It does not require much of your efforts. Certain elements compose them. Your mind gets influenced and build them up using experience and feedback on it. The mind becomes automated and fuelled with habits. Picking a tea flavour in the morning may be a very tricky business. Unless you automate it to save mental energy, so decisions are made automatically. It saves energy and time.

No matter it is a dilemma, trilemma or whatemma, people need to make decisions every day. When questions finally create the platform to execute whatemmas, one progresses with every decision taken. Things get done without giving a second thought. The automation liberates mental energy. Then the mental power goes to more sophisticated matters. Once the standard is designed - the framework is there. Like a stadium for decisions to fly. Every rule is as well as questionable as well as open to improvement.

An important note is that questions are not only for designing the standard. They automate things to decide on them with lower time and energy cost. Time and energy are resources which once depleted waste the life and reduce your focus. Instead of standing in front of the dilemma or whatemma, the standard decides whether something is good enough. What is not - gets out of frame and saves time and energy.

However, there is a popular idea that having high standards significantly contribute to misery. The truth is this. The hight of the standard reduces the supply of options accordingly. Having high standards may have zero things to pass it. Perhaps this is the unhappy situation. High standards seek for the most elegant options where minor ones are neglected. If someone is unhappy with the standard one holds, one can craft or redesign them with questions.

Everybody can question the standard. The use of questions is never limited as long as it brings utility. Even if they are useless - only you can define them. Standards for decisions are the platform. They are like a court to do justice. In this case, it is your mind to make decisions in the face of whatemma. Standards are filters for excellence. Having zero standards equates to the absence of defined worth. The lack of standard does not tell what is right and wrong, excellent or ordinary, beautiful or ugly. That is where it could bring the confusion when complexity comes in because there is no scale to measure things. Lower standards increase the supply of options and complexity with it.

Some have high standards while others are low maintenance. Having high standards set higher demands to satisfy them. Having high standards is as important as having low ones. Low standards bring little barrier for the incoming complexity. Perhaps having low standards bring more options. But at the same time, lower standards could bombard the mind with complexity of possibilities what leaves the noise, overthinking, distraction and indecisiveness.

Having higher standards serve like a filter of the incoming things. Standards better up judgements despite they could be entirely automatic. Establishing standards of excellence show only excellent ideas to the mind, so it remains undistracted by abundance. Excellent things depend on definition. Standards filter out what does not comply with the rule. If it is whatemma - it gets clarified. However, if standards are too high, eventually it filters things so acutely that nothing may come to attention because things are not good enough. That could be the road to unhappiness to someone.

Lower standards are not worse than high ones. They just put less demand on incoming things to the mind. That is where minds get confused because information may be overwhelming. If there is no standard or poorly defined one, the mind will get bombarded by information and complexity until mental energy gets depleted. What low standards can do better than high ones is they guarantee the supply of alternatives. The way leading to complications, but supply is guaranteed.

On the one hand, low standards have an abundant supply of options, but make decisions harder. On the other hand, high standards make decisions easier, but lower down the supply of alternatives where it could be absolute zero. When there is a zero incoming, there is no foundation for any decision. Again, some people are always repeating that having high standards is the road to misery. Then things are not good enough, not beautiful enough, etc. Following this attitude makes happiness a distant goal. Depending on the definition of happiness. Definition forms the standard. No matter the level of the standard. What you can do is to challenge the rule and design one for yourself. Designing your standard is a brighter option than being dissatisfied by following the given one. Questions would demonstrate their utility. The defined standard makes important things more natural to cross the finish line.

Low standards guarantee quantity, high standards stand for quality. It has never been a secret that having a low barrier for options, complexity may come in. Both quantity and quality are in need to make a decision. To choose among alternatives - there must be some alternatives, so the supply is needed. To pick something of value it shall not be too many, so it must be a defined worth that separates good from the rest.

One thing is crucial. Although standards are perfect mediators in decision making, confusing standards confuse. The decision of what is beautiful, truth standards are not for the equation. Deciding on what is the truth, utility standards are out of frame. Judging on what works, beauty standards are out of question. Just three to mention where dimensions and playgrounds are different. If someone tries to improve the functionality of something while measuring how it looks would not find what one is looking for. Standards are for different playgrounds.

Like in chess, winning moves are made not those loved personally - graceful movements are not always for winning. Winning in football is not because of the skin colour of the team, but for the skill to play football. Equally, in cooking, not the tallest person is the best cook, but the one who cooks the best. You get the idea of different standards in various platforms - different metrics to measure actions. However, you can integrate standards into a complex picture on the multidimensional fabric. There are many playgrounds - each of them have its standards.

The quest there is to challenge standards for better decisions. What matters more than the rule is the skill to make questions. They with the mind behind can dress and undress standards.

Questions make standards as well as break them down. The aim is to question and challenge this platform of justice if it is mindless or not enough for betterment. You need to make them clear. Rules are servants to make decisions on your behalf. The quest is to form or challenge standards to better them up.

Time is limited, so spending it to unimportant or irrelevant things steals it. Once time gets trumpeted as a valuable resource, people would not trade it at a low price. The famous proverb tells us that time is money. Making decisions require some. Decisions take time, so they cost. The troubling matter comes when no decision is made, but time still goes with nothing in the end. Making no choices at all is the loss. Deciding depletes, execution brings outcomes. That could be a separation between hesitation and initiative. Everybody can be in the process of deciding. If it takes ages - the mode not as decisive as you may think.

Decisions are like a bicycle - they do not move you forward unless you are pedalling this metaphor according to your standard. Not only time is limited. Energy to make decisions is limited as well. No matter big or small they are open to automation which is a natural consequence in forming a habit of deciding on your behalf. Generally, people do many little things without giving any regard to it. For example, breakfast, dressing up or a daily commute could become a habitual experience once they get automated. Habits do not demand much of the mental energy. When energy is saved, it could go to the most productive fields. Originality is greedy - it requires full engagement.

The absence of the standard for the mind potentially leads to overthinking or distraction. Unnecessary information interrupts and brings doubts. Among many alternatives, you decide where not to pay attention because some options do not satisfy your standards. Indecisiveness is the problem - the question is the solution because they develop specific standards steadily or rapidly. Otherwise, alternatives will overwhelm someone with no rule. The stricter the standard, the lower the input. Once it becomes set, it makes decisions and pushes for consequences.

Finally, having many alternatives causes paralysis in decision making. On paper, nobody wants it to happen, but practice brings a perfect condition for complexity. Unless you have your standards of selection. Time is the resource, so every delayed decision costs time. The funny thing is that nobody can repurchase it. Time gets wasted every time complexity occupies the floor. Overthinking uses energy and leads to activity with no action. That is one particular problem many will face. Questology is the answer to cure this cancer.

The Problems

> *"No problem can stand the assault of sustained thinking."*
> **Voltaire**

Indecisiveness is one problem among many others. And you cannot solve them all. The priority dictates its authority. You do not mind unimportant things to you. You pay attention to what matters. It is almost a maxim. To accelerate progress and advancement of any field, you will be forced to solve some problems. Either by necessity or by choice. As the world is imperfect, there will always be something to do. Then, another practical fundamental of progress is there. Problems - their presence is universal.

There would always be problems, tragedies or slight inconveniences - just shades of distinct intensity to define problem's identity. Having nowhere to live or nothing to eat is a more intense version of having your fridge empty. In one way or another situation can be fixed. However, more intense problems will take more time to solve them. Light ones are resolved immediately. Either you face tragedies or inconvenience - both are problems. The difference in shade does not change the nature of the problem. You solve problems, or they solve you. You cannot escape them for long. Throwing them away brings them back like the gravity pulls planets. You decide which ones are to be solved and which ones neglected. Like a priority game.

Problems are unavoidable, but if you solve them, you perfect the world and make it less faulty. Perfection is the result of faultless presence. Questology is not a blindfolded walk in the spring - it makes the world less bleak. Who has the power to think - ask questions to solve problems. This chapter institutes the universal presence of the problem itself. After all, solutions are desired where thinking is required. The universality of problems provides a panoramic playground. Questology is the key to unlock the problem like a chest.

Questions find the problem and solve it. The practical fundamental of progress is the problem, not a solution. Nobody can have a solution if there is no problem. If it would be opposite ask yourself what a solution alone intends to solve. The problem is the master to cause you a beautiful disaster. One can solve nothing but it. Moreover, you will find a good metaphor for the solution being a key to unlock chests.

A problem is like one. Unlocked and unpenetrable until the key is found. The solution to a problem is like a key to a chest. Questions design the solution out of various answers posed by minor questions. However, it is not having a right key to unlock the chest. The "right" key may not fit the chest. In contrast, the correct key is which fits the chest not which is entitled to be right. Fitness may conflict with entitlement.

When you unlock more mysteriously metaphoric chests, you have more treasure to enrich everything around. The question is the answer to many problems regardless of the shade of difficulty. Rarely anybody wants problems, but the truth is - they are inevitable. Some people tend to complain or give up. Much more clever is to embrace questions to find out the solution and crack them.

Problems are the universality. Raising up awareness of this issue wins half of the battle. A part of the population has a habit to hide or escape from problems. It is not a winning battle. Recognising problems is a direct sign of useful sight. Such is the half of the battle against the issue. Problems are not friendly to bring comfort and good company.

Solving them is another half of the battle. The question there is a starting point to look for two things in this warfare. The question finds out the problem, and the question discovers the solution. When two halves join together, they advance the current state.

The problem hiding exercise is the explanation for why problems remain. What is clear that both solving and hiding the problem require mental energy. What is similar - in both cases the problem disappears. What is different - hidden problem vanishes temporarily while resolved one permanently. Solved problems make the world less inconvenient. Refraining to solve them will do you either nothing or drain your joy. This makes hiding problems practically impractical. That is why the key to solve a problem shall be discovered with the logic in quest.

Commitment to solve problems is the progressive sign. Even missing to find the immediate solution, commitment remains accelerating. To solve problems, they must be visible to the mind's eye. For example, to fix up the car, it must be a car broken in front of you. Problems need to be in the field of vision. If there is no car, there is no problem of a broken car - the solution is out of frame then. Questions serve the compass to discover a challenge at first. The question there wins half of the battle. It shows a problem to the mind. For the final act, there is a strike to conclude with a solution.

When it comes to a general framework, one thing shall be clear. It is not necessary to have a tragedy. Even a slight imperfection will cause inconvenience. Think of delayed flights, empty fridge or dying battery - sort of inconvenience. Even such minor problems interrupt plans and intentions. To eliminate inconvenience means to solve the problem. When your phone runs out of energy - charging it solves the issue. The world is full of such small flaws. "Where is the charger?" - Leads the mind one step forward to cure a dying battery. Questology is the starter to solve problems regardless of their difficulty. It represents the compass guiding to the solution of a light or massive problem.

In this version, questions find the problem and find out the solution - the coin with two sides. Rarely anybody finds things without searching. Questions there fulfil both parts of the framework. Some people have nothing, so having problems sounds like ownership of strange property. Having problems is one thing and solving out is another one to complete the equation. If you do not see problems, you do not address them. Unfortunately, if you have troubles and you do not see them, then problems solve you.

Problems are inevitable - such is the framework and playground you must play in. Dealing with problems is a point of contract you signed up before you get born. There are plenty of ways to interact with them, but what is unhealthy is ignoring the contract. Problems will catch you - probably it is a natural charm of yours to attract them. It is enough to solve nothing to accumulate the wealth full of challenges. The central question would be how to deal with inevitability. The answer is with flair and flexibility. More than you want to solve problems. They may have an equal desire to solve you.

Therefore, problem solving is universal - solving your problem is particular. Sometimes it requires to be critical. A specific shade of mental hostility against them. Detrimental politeness towards a problem is not the part of the solution. Troubles sometimes are tough, so to solve them the mind needs to develop its toughness as well. In fact, you may find several ideas on how to solve problems or approach them critically, but one of them is very straightforward. To deconstruct the situation mercilessly. When the problem gets shattered into as many pieces as needed to be defeated - it is already the beginning of the solution.

The truth is, problems increase in complexity what makes them difficult to detonate. They evolve as well as humans do. They get harder and harder every time. When problems grow, the sophistication of mind needs to match complexity. When you look at the past, some problems seem to be evident and primitive. If someone reads history, problems of the past do not seem so tricky looking from the current standpoint. They are already solved what automatically brings you a little struggle to repeat the solution once it is learnt. However, what worked in the past does not necessarily work in the present. Why?

For example, you may remember the story of how the Ancient Greek conqueror - Alexander the Great - solved the Gordian knot. An unsolvable problem. Gordian knot resembled what had no beginning and no end. The question is how to solve the unsolvable. It was not such for Alexander - he took his sword, stroke the knot and this way untangled the sophistication in no time. Sounds simple. He conquered the known world at the time. It worked for Alexander and for a specific situation in a specific time. The effectiveness of it in modern times gets questioned. Just imagine everyone is smashing swords anywhere. To resolve a disagreement with the neighbour a sword will not help. Otherwise, it may lead to where one is dead and another - in prison. Solutions of the past may not match problems now.

So once the mind stumbles upon any problem, the solution shall match a problem like a glove matches the hand. This context requires for the answer designed for the problem. You and everyone else will reapply previous methods which worked out. It is effective until it is not. The message there would be seeking for the optimal solution. A hint for innovation of current methods. There will be the time where known models will not work for problems at hand. Then, it is smart to start from basics again. A solution is being forged til it fits the problem. Solving the problem is the second part of the game after the problem is found.

Solving problems advances the situation. For example, in business, finding out a problem and finding out the solution may make you fortune. In medicine, finding out a problem and finding out the solution extend patient's life. No matter the field - all of them have imperfections. Finding and solving them out advances. Questions act like agents to solve problems and contribute to progress. Exploration is the starting point for the discovery. Questions are for both. Questions initiate the action to unlock what is locked.

Eventually, when you rely on the chest metaphor, it is for crashing complexity that problems will fall like shattered pieces of glass. Finding a solution means understanding the structure and inserting a fitting key. It is always the thing to know how problems are made. Questions alone are pointless, while the chest without a key is useless. When both meet at place, questions are used, and the chest brings points. Understanding the structure of problems is the way to deconstruct and solve it.

Critical approach and not politeness towards tough problems is the ticket out. The critical thinking is the transition. Many would discuss far and wide its scope while it has a very elegant definition. Critical thinking equates to objective analysis. This is a combination of two very crucial elements. First, the objective will always be apart from your opinions or feelings. Second, analysis deconstructs the complicated thing into as many pieces as needed for the problem to be defeated. There critical thinking comes in impersonal and deconstructive mode. Plenty of problems are in the air, but only a tiny fraction of them are yours. Who else can solve them if not you?

The truth about problem solving is that problems get solved sooner or later. In this context, the question is something which will guide the mind from the problem to the solution as if it had an invisible, but visible link. There is the force where the compass of the mind guides you to find out the answer, or in this case - the solution. Some problems solve themselves no extra effort is needed. Sometimes problems are just imaginary, so they vanish as soon as critical thinking touches the ground. The solution finalises the case like the answer is closing a question. That is the pattern.

Complexity of the problem hides the pattern you will probably find out before cracking it. To solve a problem is to kill the structure of the problem what makes it alive. To understand the intricate patterns of the problem, an organisation of mind shall match complexity of the problem. Finding the pattern and solving it kills the problem. Patterns are tremendous assistance in solving problems.

In this case, there are two parts of its making - finding a problem and finding a solution. One's sight shall be well trained for such discoveries. Critical thinking disassociates from emotions and opinions. To deconstruct anything, you must see elements of complexity. That is where understanding of patterns gets noticed. Patterns in problem solving are like standards in decision making. While standards align complexity of the world to standards, patterns deconstruct such complexity mercilessly. What you can hardly avoid are repetition and patterns. Your behaviour and thinking are patterned as well. Unfortunately, not in a patent office.

The pattern matters a lot in solving problems. They have complexity patterned invisibly. When you find the design of the problem, you will deconstruct it. Look at it from another angle. The problem is like a virus - both have their structures. To solve a problem is to crash the structure because structures make things work. Patterns are structural, so finding the design of the problem and killing it sends the problem to the graveyard. Problems are always inevitably alive where attacks on their constitution increase the mortality to end up with a solution.

The Leadership of the Question

> *"Not all those who wander are lost."*
> **J.R.R Tolkien**

The leadership of the question is not as universal thing in a way decisions, and problems are. It has another unusual characteristic - questions lead the mind. Leadership is not a passive business in general. Questions activate your mind to make decisions, solve problems or anything you like. Questions will lead conversation, organisation or information. The list of where questions are open to the application is long enough not to mention it.

An essential statement is not that leadership is necessarily dependent on people. Leadership will come in a way just asking productive questions. So building a flair to pose a question in the air leads you out to remove a dogmatic spell. Focus goes not on a perceived leader, but the question. The question leads the mind. Not a person, but the question is closer to leadership.

The brilliant mind is a better leader than a person who looks brilliant. Your mind sets up a vision towards the future while a person verbalises it. Answers are in the short or distant future. Solving problems or making decisions is the part of the process. Why to solve problems or force yourself to make decisions after all? The question designs the vision. Losing weight, earning money, visiting other countries are acts of the future. The change happens when present and the future jump into a relationship. The question will establish this relationship.

Any effort made in the present links to the future. For example, if someone wishes to travel around more countries, therefore it is the goal of the future. It is incredible that it is even talked about.

The question sets up goals which are elements of the future. Otherwise, they would not be called goals, but memories instead if you picked another time dimension. Goals and everything achievable lies in the future. The question is how to get there. The principal way goes to the future. More practical one goes into conditions where intended things happen in the future. Sounds like the distinction between principal and practical - invisible and visible.

Things vary depending on individuals, but all individuals share the tendency of having needs and wishes. The reason why it is important stands for the central statement - the leadership of the question. For someone to get what one intends equates to find out the answer how to get there. The compass of the mind serves in the leading role. Asking questions bring answers.

What may be distinct enough is where the question delegate and lead the mind. The unconventional thinking goes far from obeying the mainstream model. To expand conventional thought, the question guides beyond familiar boundaries. Questions navigate the mind to leave patterned way and go beyond that. The truth is, the mind works alone automatically. When the question enters the scene, patterns gain another shape. Questions lead the mind out of familiar patterns and refresh the picture of the future. The goal of anything is the envisioned situation in the future - the consequence. To go towards such view, questions inspire actions. Questions make the mind moving.

Moving forward, it is always a crucial moment to realise that conventional compass shows where the North is. Right directions or ones to the left, questology guides towards a different sort of North. The course of mind is the new North. Questology is the mental compass pushing the mind towards the pulling magnet. That is how the leadership of the question enters the room.

At this moment, you treat the relationship between the present and the future in two ways. The first of them tells that there is something magnetic in the future what attracts the person. The second approach says it is barely anything in the future - everything depends on achievements made in the present. Instead of an attracting magnet, actions build towards the future. To build up towards the future or to get attracted by the future - two sides of the same coin. Pushing it or be pulled by.

When it comes to such dilemma. It would surely be a pure belief expecting that there a magnet in the future pulling you there. In this way, everything you do would be already determined by something that awaits you in the future. Such view would be undoubtedly deterministic or faithful. Everything you are doing would be simple acts of discovering yourself. Like a design where you were created to fit in and realise. You deserve nothing, but what you achieve is everything. Unfortunately, future has nothing to give you unless you wish to live on the genuine hope.

Another alternative seems to be more realistic and workable. Questions involve active imagining of what will happen in the future based on what is known now. Like the play with probabilities stemming from the present. Then the perspective of the future is in progress of being built. Nothing is pulling, and there is nothing you deserve. Questions build up ideas into practice where you need to practice questions. They merely claim for leadership leading towards the brave new future. Known patterns believably determine how the future may look. So instead of the magnet, your mind designs the magnet to get additionally pulled by it. That is the purpose of the established purpose.

There is an establishment of expectations. Experts use models to predict how specific events will develop. The only reason why hordes of them may disagree on how the future looks like is that they use different patterns of thinking. Different minds are like different languages. What is evident to the engineer may be greek to the sociologist because the engineer is technical while a sociologist will be in the different mind frame. This is to display the difference. Patterns of thinking will quickly limit communication across lines. Models make things predictable that is why people love submitting to rules and norms.

In the opposite, unpredictable things are unstable and dangerous. When there are no patterns, there is no confidence and predictions. It partly explains while people are strongly tied with the comfort zone as if it was only one universe in the universe. Comfort zone protects from instability which is naturally around. Patterns give regularity for equilibrium - for everybody to stay grounded. Challenging questions are not the most welcoming guests for they rock the boat. Although the past is the past, and the future is the future, the use of patterns brings a foundation to build up a question for any initiative. The leadership of the question builds upon the stable ground to expand.

That is where questions shape the future. The question leads out of pattern although it stands on the pattern. They contribute to the mind to go forward. Without them, it would stand still and follow the rules which tell what to do. The future is the place where are no consistent patterns yet. The mind is not left for a repetitive pattern, but for itself. Questions are to expand or challenge limits to delegate the mind to something.

A closed mind is finite leaving little room for more fulfilment. To open up the mind, one needs to break up boundaries of repetitive patterns. Not a violent act, but questions navigate from the consistency towards improvement. The question leads the mind to connect with novelty to gather new experience. Then to think, do and speak things which are not thought, done or spoken so far begins with the question for a starter.

People will retain wants and needs, so they will need answers. If there is any need or desire, there is the apparent scarcity of such things. Lack means they are not there now. So fulfilment looks like the answer lies in the future. There must be something to expect anything. If we speak practically, questions and execution are what brings the future to the present, and questions lead the mind from the present to the future.

To question is to break the glassy end of the pattern to see more than the pattern defines. Systems are everywhere, so the world is a very complicated place. If you see any element - it is ruled by the force which is described in the system. Your habits are the system to start from. To break them out, pattern shall get fragile to replace one habit to another. Thinking patterns are of the same kind. The question finds out the problem and question finds the solution - this is also a pattern. It creates a relationship between the present and the future. The question may challenge the model to go towards the future. That is mainly what leadership of the question is all about - leading the present to the future.

Questions are to navigate the mind beyond known patterns. There is always to see something new. For the mind to advance questions need to dance. Everybody has standards and patterns to act. Standards align your decisions and make them happen. Patterns predict things if they follow the model. One needs to jump into motion where the dancing metaphor is the thought explosion. Accepting the leadership of questions is one of many suggestions.

What you need is to ask questions. Not for everybody else. Not for the vague concept of progress or betterment, but yourself first. The leadership of the question pushes your mind forward. Your patterns grow in variety, and your standards experience novelty. For a better replacement, you find different patterns or standards to adopt. The question is a swift shift in your mental script.

Chapter 3:
The First Principle of Questology:
The Question-Answer Bridge

The question structures and at some degree predicts answers.

People may wonder why to ask questions - because they bring answers. Those you need. Asking what you want is a good start. Knowing why you want what you want is a beautiful upgrade. Knowing how to accomplish what you want brings majestic finalisation. Having some questions is not enough. What you generally need are answers. Results depend on executing questions rather than having them in the first place. Questions delegate the mind to the future, bring the sense of purpose and target to reach.

The connection of question and the answer acts similarly like the reason causes a result. Straightforwardly defined. So the very first principle of questology attempts to establish a permanent link. The condition where questions act like starters and answers - like finishers. People need specific answers, but what matters is the question.

Generally, answers close the gap while questions target things. The main aim is to realise that questions and answers stay in the permanent bond. Like seeing the relationship between the present and the future. Some things are more difficult than others that is why not all questions are answered quickly. But all of them have answers. Even wrong answers are answers after all.

Questions are in search of something incredible. Sometimes new and useful. Often someone is looking for meaning, entertainment, success or whatever. If that someone does not find what one looks for - it stems in the form of the invention of sense, designing pleasant activities or building success. People are inventive. When questions target the future, questions go like shot of the arrow - it lands somewhere. The capital thing is to act upon it. Actions fulfil them until it becomes realised. The leadership of the question makes the mind to stumble upon something sensible, valuable and unique.

Generally, everyone wants something - a fundamental statement to put questology into context. There, wants and needs are present intentions to be ended in the future. The relationship between the present and the future as if they were inseparable. For the sake of example, if today is Monday and someone wants to dine on Friday, therefore the plan is set. Such an idea did not exist before the establishment of the intent.

If you do not want, you do not dine on Friday. There, wants influence and predict actions in the future. Wants are powerful enough to summon the picture of the future. Wants are not enough; the effort is needed as well. This quickly establishes the relationship between the present and the future. Motivation lies seeing this relationship. That is how the perspective is born.

Understanding this basic thing is an advantage of applying questology. If there is nothing in the future - no plans, visions, hopes, duties or whatever - there are no incentives to solve problems and make decisions because they guide nowhere. Level of optimism is unbearably low. Lack of perspective makes everything blind. A hopeless case is like a blindfolded walk in the spring. Many exciting things of which the blindfolded one cannot see.

Questology provides a perspective by default. The question inflicts the future automatically. The question is built on real understanding which draws the picture on the future. That is how attitude develops. By a sheer amount of learning and asking questions, the future is created in mind. What is needed is the work to make mental into practical.

The future is invisible if the person does not see it. Despite being surprisingly unpredictable, future is there. Someone may say that there is no future. Time would have frozen down, and nothing would have happened. Today would have never come if you thought of it yesterday. If there is no future - tomorrow will never come. You decide on how believable it is.

However, the world runs on probabilities and never provides something sure. Possibilities are hope in numbers. Even the most certain statement - your dinner at 7 pm - may not happen because many things can influence the change of events. What is taken for sure will score the highest likelihood, but never the certitude because the world runs on probabilities. Like a game.

Although future runs on probabilities and is in the relationship with the present, there are two ways to look at this. One is the principal, and another is practical. The principal level is invisible, inaudible and untouchable. The practical level is opposite - it is visible, audible and touchable. For the sake of example, gravity pulls things down, but you do not see the principle. What you will see are things falling. Also, you do not hear gravity, but you hear how plates hit the floor. This throws a hint about different dimensions - visible and invisible. We act upon what is practical using what is principal. Your habits are principal, but things you do with them are practical. You will find it familiar.

Principally, the future exists despite your wishes because time is not frozen. The simple pattern of time transition imposes the necessity of incoming moments. On the main ground, if you remember yesterday now, why should not you remember this moment tomorrow? A natural transition of time with the past-present-future scheme is there. In this context, it would have no reason to think about this scheme if time was frozen. Then no change would be possible, so that the future would be impossible. Tomorrow is like gravity - you might not see it, but it is there. This is the principal level.

Practically, the future does not exist until you create it. Quite the opposite, is not it? Just think about people of previous centuries. It was not apparent to them what you take for granted now. Show a smartphone to any medieval king, and you would get hanged for practical sorcery. Things you use are practical, factual and they are there. That is the moment of confidence. We trust in things we see, hear and touch. They bring us data to think about. Someone may see the present moment as the consequence of past data. Future has no data to think about. That is a certain point to disbelieve in it, so questions are there to build the picture of the future first. The principal is the more significant concern in this book. After all - we act upon what is practical using what is principal.

The reason why we involve the fusion of the principal and practical is that the question-answer bond is principal. Something you cannot see, hear or touch, but you can use it. As the element belonging to a different category, this link is something to be sensed mentally. Practically, the future does not exist until you create it. Principally, there is the future. Therefore, there is a gap in mind to design the future and accomplish it. The simple example is to set a goal on Monday to dine on Friday. Voila, the future is created. This plan did not exist before your design. Questions there are to target the time in the future where the answer lies. The question always connects with the answer. That is the bond.

Some answers are immediate, and some require more time. The question about weather is brief while how to find the answer to the world's poverty may take a little longer. Easy questions hit the answer almost immediately. Weather conditions are checked and answered in the blink of an eye. Harder questions require more time and sophistication to untangle complexity. They take more time because they are uneasy. Questions like perpetual peace, an extension of wellbeing to increase health and wealth are completely random, but too complex to get solved immediately. To accomplish something, someone needs to initiate. The question is a perfect starter to build a bridge to connect the island of the present with the island of the future.

The bond has the beginning which looks like a question. Although the link not made of the finest metal - steel or titanium - it has the mental toughness. Not material, yet, you cannot shatter it anyway because it is based on logic. Questions point at answers like the present heads towards the future. Immaterial and unbreakable sounds bizarre, and it is logical. Logic is what gives all the confidence. Opinion is common, logic is rare. Therefore, it is logic you should find yourself on rather than trust in opinion. It makes logic a valuable resource on the planet because it is in the DNA of critical thinking. The scarcity of reason makes critical thinking so high in demand and low in supply now. Logic is rare, metallic and it works. Use it - it is common property.

Following this, logic is mental - you cannot see, hear or touch it. But you can use and sense it. What you see, hear or touch will be metal. That is the difference between what is practical and what is principal. Metal is real; mental is surreal. Metal is material; mental is immaterial. Metal is physical, mental is intellectual. Metal is weighty, mental is lightweight. Metal is framed, mental is the framework. Everyone finds the structure in the metal, but the bond is where you will find the mental structure. You will see the mind when it is put into metal. So you act upon what is practical using what is principal.

The link which is between the question and the answer is what this principle is all about. The link is principal while the length is practical. The length is unknown, but predictable. Asking questions is like shooting the arrow - it lands somewhere. Extracted answers start directly or with most silent intention. Usually, people do not pay attention to things they do not care about - answers are intentionally charged. So if the answer is found, it is based on the intention. Direct or indirect one.

Questions and answers are linked principally. That is why it is the first principle of questology after all. Structure binds them together like a mental bridge of two points to build a comfortable relationship between the present and the future. This is the clear picture to establish trust in the usefulness of questions. Admittedly, it is easier to see the London Bridge crossing Thames than reading about something you cannot see or touch. The important part is that you understand this bond even if you are unable to estimate its length. Although it is tricky to say when someone will get to the answer. The bond is more straightforward - it starts with questions to finish with answers. Seeing this link allows to exercise the trust in the future.

If you take another expression of the bond. Every ship has the distance to conquer before it reaches the port. Some are far; some are short. Some are like Rotterdam and London, others like L.A. and Shanghai. It corresponds with weighty and lightweight questions. Some are answered immediately or require some effort. The question-answer bridge in the framework is so unbreakably logical. This link is like the route connecting two cities. The question connects with the answer like Rotterdam connects with London.

Since you leave Rotterdam, you know you will reach London if you sail there. The question brings a perspective and confidence to ask more questions to complete your initiative.

Once started, only the destination point is foggy. Length hides in the fog. A straightforward formula builds up execution on your questions to strike through the curtain of doubt. The bond there is one of many ways to establish your focus and clarity of mind. That is the mental bridge. Length is unknown, but the bridge is there.

If you want another analogy - the question triggers a gunshot - a bullet lands somewhere. Such landing spot is the answer. If someone does not take a shot, consequences remain in the trigger. Verbalising a question resembles a gunshot charged with the intention to get the answer. Then asking questions inspires for focus on answers necessarily.

Finally, the link there is like a signal. Like in communication networks, thinking line is similar. In communication, the message gets broadcast and received. Two points are needed. This analogy represents the bond between the question and the answer. To ask a question and receive a response is similarly like the journey of the signal. Perhaps answers do not come as straight as the message goes, but it travels to the intended destination in the straightest mode possible.

These analogies are to display the indestructible link where the question and the answer are connected. Hopefully, it brings a better understanding to see the invisible. That is the primary concern of the first principle. Knowledge of the bond gives the confidence in making questions because they connect with answers, accomplishments, and knowledge you need.

Chapter 4:
Translating present to the future
By putting future into present

> *"The best way to predict the future is to create it."*
> **Abraham Lincoln**

We know times in history when the world knew little about America since Europeans started their sea voyages and discovered it. Once people did not know how to escape Earth's atmosphere til they landed on the Moon. Curiosity led to discoveries and accomplishments. When you think of this, it seems evident to us because it happened. It was not so obvious for those who started going into the unknown until the question found out the answer. The question penetrated the smoke of unknown. What was unknown to the previous generations is learnable now. What is not known about the future now, will become learnable in the future.

Eventually, the question is the starter - the answer is the finisher. The question is intentional while answer tends to close up. To invent the future means to bring up the answer which fills the gap. What widens the gap are untaken decisions and unsolved problems. What closes it are decisions taken and problems solved. It is harder to fill the gap if there is no answer. The question is the start to deal exclusively with problems and decisions you cannot avoid for long. When you can decide - you move forward. Equally, the problem solved makes struggling things moving. Questology steps in as the initiator and the achiever because questions initiate while answers achieve - questology is for this relationship.

For the bond - it is in the framework. The place where the question and the answer belong to different time dimensions - they are not at the same time. So to speak, when someone asks a question at the moment - answer comes later. That is why they are not at the same time and place. That is to say about the relationship between the present and the future. It becomes relevant since you ask questions to derive new knowledge. Answers will lead to discoveries and inventions if questions guide towards it. The first principle of questology, the link connecting your initiative with achievement. If questions strive to connect with something else - they will find the closing point.

As you extract the relationship between the question and the answer, you will step forward to think about futuristic implications. Like the ship leaving Rotterdam will arrive in London, so the present will come in the future. The new link to extend. In fact, when you think of any complicated question, you will not know the answer immediately if you have never learnt it in books. When the answer is not immediate, it hides in the future. The question explores it mentally first and builds it practically second. Or not.

The logic in quest starts the movement to fulfil the link and arrive at the answer, solution, decision, accomplishment, happiness, satisfaction, excitement or anything you want. When the question starts the movement - the answer ends it. Only time is unknown. Future is sometimes distant. Then questions become more of a ship conquering long distances through the sea of complexity. The question-answer relationship is what you need to keep in your mind. If any of the perspectives do not fit you - ask your questions. Questions design the gravity for answers.

The question is the starter - think about progress. Things do not change unless they start. The question is the first-rate initiator of everything. That is why it claims for leadership. Not only questions set up the future. Needs are something to determine it. Everyone needs something. Future gets influenced by them. You will get thirsty, hungry or tired. With extreme conviction, anybody will tell you that you will eat, drink or sleep soon. Otherwise, you will die. No reason to bother. Basic biological needs are patterned, so they demand fulfilment. Otherwise, such systems die or suffer. To maintain biological systems functioning, one complies with needs. Accomplishment brings energy for the function. The reason why we mention biology is that it works on patterns which strongly influence the short-term future. This part is predictable.

Sometimes people want things they do not need, and they need things they do not want. Wants are not necessary to survive, but they are hardly replaceable to thrive. There is where the mindset builds upon biological hardware. Wishes are more intentional and less fixed. Sometimes, people want luxe cars when they do not need them. Contrastingly, people need to keep healthy when they do not necessarily want to eat healthily or stay fit. Such distinction is quite intricate to display the connection between what is essential.

In this context, biology and the mindset are something standing for needs and wants. The mindset is more comfortable to bend; biology is hardwired. They play the symphony for the future - needs and wants slightly influence the picture of it. The mindset empowers biology and biology supports your mindset. We face up the power of needs and desires they press on everyone. There are many areas where invisible matches visible.

What we care about is to transcend the limitations of human biology. There comes the mindset - a minor upgrade for it. While needs influence the future, wants and inclinations contribute to inventing it. Questions are the capital locomotive for the future. Answers change the game, but to find them out, first of all, you need to ask.

Symphony is a play. What is vital about questions is that they will steer needs and wants to influence the future. They are not only to be themselves, but to influence the system. It is not new that your habits are carrying you somewhere. Changing habits change the future. Habits are patterned, so questions there could redesign the future on this level. There, questions challenge and manage patterns presented by needs and wants. In this way, questioning could get an immediate impact on the future. The start to change habits and manage wants - guide you somewhere accordingly. Change requires decisions - the question assists in arriving there. Change requires a solution - questioning unlocks the problem.

Questions are formed on demand. If you do not need or want anything, the mind has no incentives to question things to better up. To design the future one needs to build it. Future manifests itself as the result of a present effort. Tomorrow is not factual - it is only a mental picture first. The future is at least a few moments from now. Past was moments ago. You will learn history, but can you learn the future? It would be a breakthrough if the future would be as learnable as the past. There is a plot twist.

To learn anything, it must be known to a sensible degree. It may sound ludicrous to learn what does not exist - the future. Past is documented to bring some facts. Future is futuristic, not factual. To make future learnable, the first question to answer is how to discover the unlearnable. For example, many will learn now specifications of existing smartphones. Smartphones you have now did not exist some decades ago. Just think how someone from the late 60s learns those specifications - they did not exist, so they were unlearnable. Developments in technology have led to the situation we have now. Progress does not slow down. The question is how to discover the future first, so to make it learnable to others after.

You understand yourself that future is not the member of learnable facts. Not many even aspire to translate current knowledge towards the future. Pressures of current events may be causing enough trouble even to think about it. The future does not belong to the real world what drops a hint why it is neglected by many. Rarely people spend on "learning" the future because it did not happen. Like winter is coming every year, so the future does the same.

The past is the perfect area for learning. Plenty of data there to be learnt because it happened. For example, you imagine historical periods or things you did yesterday. Facts are recorded, so everyone can gather knowledge of this. Future only gets factual when it becomes the past. You do not know what is coming in four years from now. It becomes evident after five years pass by. The person merely outlives the period which is the future now, but will become the past later. That is to say about learnability.

Future vanishes every moment because part of it becomes the past. Time is limited - it is like a cigarette burning the present off leaving its vivid ashes to the past. Future is what we got left to be built. History is the lesson. Some people prefer to live in the lesson over and over again while the rest learns it and moves forward. A forward-looking approach is what separates futurist from someone living in the past.

Questions are born in the present, answers are in the future, but you will learn from the past. In fact, you will direct your attention to look at things from various perspectives. Like being on the elevated ground where someone will watch Southwards or Northwards. In the same timescale, you will see the future or turn your attention to the past. What is the ground you hold this point of view? Present.

Any learning involves knowledge and its applications. Future may be imaginary or assumed in the first place. Once the picture is set, comes the time to execute it by bringing future to reality. Future is unknown. So bringing it to reality means deriving something new from the old according to the standard. You will learn what is invented or discovered. To create or discover is to derive what is unknown entirely. Merely to find the answer to a particular question while others cannot. The answer which works and makes things better.

To imagine the future, one travels in time mentally. Time is never a frozen moment. Many can travel time mentally. It is enough to think today of tomorrow, and your mind is in the future. Tomorrow will be today and today will be yesterday. Time is never a frozen moment. Why is it important? Because the mind will jump to the future and bring it faster than it comes naturally. The mental picture of the future excels the reality. Realising such picture makes futuristic things "learnable." What is learnable gets practical. The future is not realistic because it is not learnable yet. But if someone jumps there and brings it to the present, then it is another story.

Indeed, we have an assumption that the future is unlearnable. Having ambitions to learn the future is quite a tricky business in general. Imagine how the future would look after 60 seconds. A very close one. It does not promise much to change, but the time has begun. When you take this mental example, you start counting and time goes by. The movement begins with one and finishes at 60 - nothing complicated. The reason for this example is that you will easily envision future after 60 seconds. Not a significant change between now and then, but you see the relationship.

Moreover, a thought-provoking part comes when you start amplifying your perception. Perhaps you can envision future which is farther in time than 60 seconds. For example, how the change will be in one hour, a day, a week, one month, etc. Only time is multiplied. Future remains future. Having 60-second thought experiment, it seems that you will learn future almost effortlessly. It seems that you almost know what will happen in those

60 seconds, then what? Then you either flow with time or go ahead of it. Counting goes with the flow, jumping ahead those 60 seconds is moving mentally faster than the time goes. The jump could be amplified as well. The mind jumps in time or goes with it.

Having this 60 seconds thought experiment you challenge the assumption that the future is unlearnable. Future is learnable because you almost know what will happen after those 60 seconds. Learnable in another way. In strict terms, either the future is in 60 seconds or the future in 60 years - it is future after all. Only distance is the difference. You even do not need to jump into complex probabilities to predict because the future is near. If you learn future in 60 seconds, it means that you will learn amplified future, right? Not necessarily. The farther the future, the less accurate the prediction.

The problematic element comes because future runs on probabilities. Even if you take a brief period of 60 seconds - something unexpected may happen. Someone may knock the doors or an unexpected phone call. Then learning could get interrupted and distorted. Not a very solid foundation of knowledge. Future carries probabilities - future runs on likelihood, not certitude. Moreover, 60 seconds journey is short. The line of time that goes from the beginning to the end. We claim the question-answer bond, and it connects moments of time. Some periods are shorter; some are longer. Equally, questions are complicated or straightforward to answer. It forms the bond bridging two points in time.

You may be jumping from one time to time just because you can. To learn the future means to create it. Execution of strategy brings future to the present. Imagination has no boundaries in the free and cultivated mind. Everyone can imagine the future, but not everyone finds the energy to act upon it to make it practically learnable. Imagination is barely practical, but practical imagination is inventive - inventions are learnable, understandable and checkable. The question is like a gunshot where the bullet lands somewhere. It is to say about consequences using flair to pose the question in the air.

The reason why we call future learnable, think about this for a moment. You set any goal - it gains its shape in the future. The panoramic view remains mental until it gets acted upon. Learning the future is principally realising the picture of mind to make it practical. Plans are in the future, but eventually, they become real when they get finished. So accomplishing the project is acting upon the future and building up. Then it becomes learnable for everyone and does not stand like a beautiful idea left without execution.

Future is not common, and common sense is not futuristic. This is a severe rebuke against the future being realistic. The more distant future, the less precise the prediction. Future is unreal because it shares little likelihood to satisfy common sense. Common sense is like a protestor against the future because it challenges common logic, traditions, and norms. Everything that associates with stability is less to do with the future - future is very unstable. The future disobeys to the logic of reality - it escapes from patterns, norms or any laws. Tomorrow has no data to get patterned. Originality, freedom and wealth are forces to put pressure on reality to extract the future. Building it up is like squeezing juice from a lemon into the glass while at the same time hoping the glass is there. That is the new learning of the future.

The vision of the future is convertible into the metaphor of the glass. Look directly, in practice you are perfectly able to pour extra water into an empty glass. You take a jug, fill it and then pour held water to the glass - it becomes fulfilled. When it comes to the future - our actions complete the picture like water fulfils the glass. The execution which is taken on questions contributes to the glass of fulfilment. For example, many exciting technologies are getting emerged. Those are like incomplete glasses because they are in the beginning. They will have many implications for everyone. For example, the Internet of things, increased lifespan or fully sustainable energy supply - just a few to mention. There is always the process of becoming. Becoming is the process to complete the glass which can never be full unless you impose the limit.

Such metaphoric glass serves for a purpose - to demonstrate a complex concept visually. Every started thing has its chance to get finished if it gets executed properly. If you stick with the example of emerging technologies, it grows into something valuable. Different stages of development are quite familiar. Some technologies are in research, others - in distribution. Futuristic vision is like the metaphoric empty glass. It does not exist in any form unless efforts fill some water in it. Above all, the future is like an empty glass you complete with answers you derive from questions. That is why seeing the glass is equally as important as filling one. Otherwise, the future would remain as a beautiful idea only. Questions reveal the glass. Your effort completes the picture. Tomorrow is the picture at first, but the execution and the work translate it into practice.

Vision is the naked strategy in the absence of tactics. Execution dresses up the concept. Knowledge and insight will always find the most creative picture of the future. Vision is the most civil rebellion against reality because it transcends the present moment. Future is just a different present where it is unreal now while reality is authentic. Reality is backed up with data where future is not. Such is just an idea yet where to make it practical you will need to sweat.

To make future learnable means to transform its vision into the present. That is the place where futuristic may equate to practical. It becomes not only realistic, but also accessible to everyone. It stops being just an idea, but gains its physical shape instead. The city built, the art created or technology developed - something achieved. Before doing this, it is often wise to visualise the road. What city to build, how to create art or why build to technology - just some questions to imply answers. What matters, in the end, are answers. Those are the future, so answers start from questions. Therefore, to build the future one needs to accept the leadership of the question and execute upon it. Questions cannot be left alone. Execution is vital to squeeze answers and bring the future to the present by pushing forward the present.

The future is coming after all. You go there from the present to the future in a way that question squeezes the answer. The point about learnability shifts its natural understanding. If you looked at the past, you would learn many things from there. For example, from books, stories or the Internet you can learn about European, American, Chinese or any other history. You can learn about the previous century in great details quickly. You can learn stories that happened, and the tricky part is to envision stories to occur. Designing the picture of the future based on the current understanding is delicate and always unstable. The world runs on probabilities, so learning the future is like the game against the chance. You can play it.

The game of chance is an interesting point though. If the opportunity to win in the lottery increases from 1% to 2% - it is a 100% increase, chance clearly doubles. Someone may brighten up for such growth. Still, the player has 98% likelihood to fail and 2% to win - just a rough example. Equally the future would have a 98% chance of not occurring as expected. Bringing the future into practice is a constant combat against the chance. Any effort made contributes to what is intended like every ticket you buy increases the chance. Every activity has chances for success and failure.

Probably is to say that even a 1% chance to win a lottery, for instance, is higher than 0%. But there is the point to question. Percent of success is low, while the chance of failure is crushingly high. Inevitably, someone before doing those things needs to examine implications. How much time and resources it may ask for every attempt. After all, there are many other things to try which are more likely to be brought from the future into practice. Or in other words, having a higher chance of success. This is the new learning - converting future into practice by translating present into the future. As if it were two languages. When you build present, you alter in some way what is already there. A simple act that receives its conversion. The mind puts pressure on the future by translating futuristic into practical. Everything is possible, yet some things are more probable than others.

Again, questions start now, and answers come later. Design of the future is workable. Perhaps the intended picture of the future is done 15%, 25%, 50% or whatever. Questions provide answers to fulfil the metaphoric glass until it reaches a workable level to convert a futuristic design into a more practical understanding. Futuristic things at the moment are unconventional because they are not mainstream. When they become familiar, they are no longer futuristic, but real. Other futuristic things emerge - other things gain their shades of unreality.

There is one critical thing while pushing the present to the future. What seems impossible, in fact, is always possible. For example, a 10% chance of success is not impossible. 1% chance of success is not impossible. 0.1% chance of success is not impossible. What you need is to look at the statistical balance and ratio to be rational. The probability of failure there is crushingly high under those circumstances, and probably you will not get involved in such unstable activities. However, impossible is possible if you look from a numeric standpoint. Every vision is possible. The question is how to win the game against the chance.

Impossible would mean probability equal to 0%. That would mean a frozen time. In case you read this - it does not apply there and anywhere. Probability compose 100% chance of a particular platform where success and failure share this pie. Advantages favour success while disadvantages contribute to failure. Impossible is just a word to refer to the most likely failure with a tiny grain of hope. Impossible does not exist. If one thinks opposite - nothing is being done because the mind is already defeated.

Many would probably want to see the future as being bright. Some of them see the future while some see no future. The pressure of the present is the substantial reason to be blind to it. Despite being pressed in the present, every problem solved, and decision made contribute in building up the future.

On the optimist note, future is better than the moment of now. The historical development gives such hint. It is enough to compare 1018, 1918 or 1998 to 2018 regarding freedom, health, wealth or whatever - the change is drastic. Is there any reason why 2038, 2118 or 3018, for instance, should be worse than 2018? You are going towards this while technology develops, economy matures, society improves. You need to build it. The civilisation augments itself with every achievement it makes.

Chapter 5:
The Second Principle of Questology:

The Mental Architecture
To upgrade a brilliant culture

> *"No great improvements in the lot of mankind are possible until a great change takes place in the fundamental constitution of their modes of thought."*
> **John Stuart Mill**

> *"We shape our buildings; thereafter they shape us."*
> **Winston Churchill**

After the signal between questions and answers is found, there is another step to make. A step to increase complexity of understanding to reduce complexity of everything. When the mind understands the complex, it does not look so complicated. Hard problems you once were solving were impenetrable to your mind. To repeat the solution, you would do it in a swift act, so the unprepared problem would not know how to react. Caught off guard. The second principle of questology is about the mental architecture. It stores your knowledge and experience, standards and patterns. Moreover, it acts as a personal government running on its logic.

Think about the castle standing near the lake. You will notice two of them - one is the original while another - a reflection on the lake surface. So reflection and the original castles drop something to consider. We transform this concept into twofold reality. One seen by eyes and another seen by mind's eye. Having this, the mental architecture looks like the imprint of the reality people start carrying with themselves. Something that creates gravity in mind where mental elements spin around in a particular order. The distinct gravity is the mental architecture - a skeleton of thinking to be dressed.

In a conventional sense, buildings are the pleasant landscape of local architecture. Every city in the world has its charm inviting visitors to experience the uniqueness. You may enjoy cities in the entire spectrum, from the Americas to Europe, From Russia to Asia. All of the continents have to offer something different. Defined by climate, culture, and history - something visible, audible and touchable. In a conventional architecture, we have an obvious thing - property. Real estate which stands somewhere - an architectural foundation with the style and structure on it.

When you jump to the mental architecture, you have mental property as well. Instead of being a matter of concrete, glass or steel, the mental architecture have other material to organise. They are experiences, thoughts, patterns, standards or anything you can think about. Such property has its centre - gravity of mind where everything thinkable will be sucked in. It is invisible, inaudible and untouchable. Like most cities have their centres, the mental architecture has its core. The rest develops outwards. The mental structure is the foundation of the city you build in yourself. Undoubtedly, the city of another dimension.

The mental architecture is a vivid picture to display rationality and design of your mind. The mind is the government after all. Principles of logic are like principles of physics. The only difference is that physics goes for the physical world, while logic stands for the mental one. Conventional architecture obeys to physics, mental one - to logic. Taking physics, you see many things falling, and you say it is due to gravity. For logic, you see many things making sense due to obedience to logic. Physical and mental worlds are very intricately connected. Laws of physics and logic are stable, yet, questionable.

The mental architecture is to institute the foundation of logic in mind. Many would say that logic connects two separate points like the immortal line in geometry. The first principle of questology manifested a single connection. The question-answer bond was the first step into complexity management. From there you develop the entire network of connections forming a structure to govern complexity in mind and the world. The framework we involve under the name of the mental architecture is ingrained in the human culture. The mode where everything connects with everything and still makes an organisation in your mind rather than chaos.

The mental architecture is a metaphor to represent the interior design where character and rationality join together. The organisation manages things going through the sea of everyday complexity. You need answers to avoid sinking in the sea of information. You have some information which is useful, and the rest is daily noise. The noise brings complications. To ask questions is not enough. Dealing with answers is another part of the story. That is why dealing with answers is equally important as asking questions. Your mind deals with things leading with the logic in quest.

The abundance of answers is common in the society where information replaces blood in people's veins. Not all answers, as well as information, are relevant. In a hyper informative society, there are more answers than you need. So in abundance, your mind will get easily distracted if it has no standard to define relevance. If someone does not know how to behave with answers, it is equal to having no answers at all. Questions do not bring their full value then. The mental architecture becomes a secret government to sail through such sea of complexity, make decisions and solve problems. It is the standard to behave with answers.

Therefore, questology is more than baking questions like cakes. Complexity penetrates the individual to cause trouble. Confusion is the result. To prevent from such end of events, the mind puts complexity into a defined structure. It is not enough to ask questions to collect answers, but to employ consequences productively. Information makes you better informed - it increases decision quality. Also, knowledge brings you extra strength in solving problems. However, if your mind fails in governing what it gets, then no answer becomes productive, and questioning will grow futile. Your mind shall succeed not only in asking questions, but in behaving with answers and information as well.

Our mind always has things to collect and to think about. Logic is often a loud word we coin to things that make sense. Sometimes people accredit everyday things to be rational because things seem smart. Even the most irrational, ludicrous and backward opinion would seem logical to someone. It is a general impression. As you already know - logic is impersonal, so any effort to call sentiments and opinions a part of logic would go out of frame.

Instead, the mental architecture is where you blend uniqueness of your character and metallic logic. You have two elements, join them together and eventually get someone like you. That is the alliance of character and rationality. Sounds very simple, but complexity hides behind. It involves many elements to make you-you. In other words, there is material and shape, content and structure, character and rationality. The reason why you need to understand this is for better reception of the mental architecture. The alliance of character and rationality is a serious question. To understand this is an excellent way to start from intricately invisible logic.

The alliance involves both agents. The character is needed because logic will give you the structure, but will never tell you what should be inserted in it. The character is necessary because logic will tell you what is missing, but will not add anything new. The character is needed because logic will show you the optimal process of making things done without ever introducing how to make things done better. Logic will criticise everything, but never create anything. Logic alone is the tool to judge, plan or think, but it is invisible. Logic cares about your sentiments as the fork cares about your taste.

Not only logic has its downsides. You perfectly know personal things are sometimes irrational, but you like them. Logic does not care about opinions while opinions repay in skipping up logic. For example, wants you have are not logical. Goals are not rational. Motivations are not reasonable. All of them are personal. Things are interesting because they are illogical. Logical things are boring.

Your personality is what finds the fit to its standards. Logic is the skeleton inside of things. Joining rationality with character is an easy task - it will not be easier than splitting the atom. However, before you join them together, you split to connect.

Material like clay gets shaped into bricks; written content gets structured into paragraphs, rationality governs the spirit of the character. There is the moment where the principal and practical meet each other. The dressing moment is perfectly illustrated when the human skeleton is dressed with flesh - the framework frames the framed. Logic is like a skeleton while your character is an authentic dress.

Firstly, for the actual connection take a very simplistic and initially irrelevant equation:

$x + y = z$

Or if you prefer numerical way:

2 + 3 = 5

Something evident because it is fundamental. Good news is if the basic composition works, it is time to advance into a more sophisticated and therefore less stable organisation. It is time to split the atom:

Human body + <u>Human psychology</u> = Human being

This follows the same basic structure, yet it conveys more meaning than previous elements. You connect two components to extract the third one - something familiar. Starting from basics is always a good start. It has the chance for a sudden expansion due to lack of complication.

Therefore, you take the basic surface of this:

Human body + <u>Human psychology</u> = Human being

To expand into this:

(**Muscular system** + **Nervous system** + **Skeletal system** + **Respiratory system** + **Circulatory system, etc.**) + <u>Human Psychology</u> = Human being

More accurately, details complicate the picture. Complexity is more obvious. Once you expanded one element, you will go further. Follow the same basic equation to play out with other elements as well:

Human body + <u>(Developmental aspect + Behavioural aspect + Social aspect + Cognitive aspect + Environment aspect, etc.)</u> = Human being

If you extracted both, then you would get something like this:

(**Muscular system** + **Nervous system** + **Skeletal system** + **Respiratory system** + **Circulatory system, etc.**) + <u>(Developmental aspect + Behavioural aspect + Social aspect + Cognitive aspect + Environment aspect, etc.)</u> = Human Being

Which is equal to

Human body + <u>Human psychology</u> = Human being

Which follows

x + y = z

Or

2 + 3 = 5

Just wondering which is less complicated. The elegant facade is often the iceberg to contain a supreme complexity. The organisation of mind is weaponry to fight against the lure of complexity which does nothing but pulls you into distraction. The mental architecture has its laws to operate against the tornado outside its yard.

Then,

Human Being = Character

And,

Character + Intelligence = Intelligent Character

Still on basic mathematical formula interchanging the content. Having two blending elements, you open up the gates to the mental architecture. The character needs mental models to operate. The mental design is like the mental architecture which joins your character. Generally, the mental architecture has its rules to get applied and things to govern. It is the secret government for solving problems and making decisions. Moreover, it is for meeting answers as they were data.

Mental models are to extend the performance of someone. The problem is the human body which has its cycle of development. It grows, matures and declines - evolution set in genes. The human body is taken care of through proper nutrition, suited fitness or other means. You will care for the body by designing specific disciplines.

The mind then will open up itself to get disciplined like your body. Few chapters will introduce laws of the mental architecture which govern the mind. To transcend the limitation of human biology depends on asking questions. Then the mind is a locomotive, and the body seems like a pulled wagon. Logic ignores human condition and acts on its own - people die, but logic is timeless.

After all, the mental architecture is for navigating in complexity. Questioning things involve answers. Someone needs manners to behave with the incoming complexity. Complexity management is an agreeable term. The mental institution is what shall solve incoming problems and eventually assist in deciding over things. The organisation is often more productive than chaos. Confusion distracts while any level of intelligence unites your mind together. Then it will recognise patterns, and structures strictly or loosely. Further laws of the mental architecture give a metallic taste of logic.

The Law of Acuity

*Never accept anything for real
if reality has something to conceal.*

We will meet a commonly held belief that the majority's vote is considered to be more right than that of minority's. In general, it is the majority of people who agree on something. It is not logic speaking but democracy where opinion is common. Opinion is unstable - the impact on the mood may change it. After, they outgrow into common sense to make better judgements. Common sense is a prudent way to get protected from silly mistakes and bring value to practical conclusions. Some people centuries ago believed that Earth is flat and that was common sense. Now, it does not look so common what makes this slightly problematic.

The good news about common sense - it gives the standard and golden rule to approach life. It stood the test of time, so it sounds like the echo of wisdom. It is always easy to follow the pattern than to question it. The mind does not rock the boat to cause fewer problems. There, patterns and habits are the embodiment of stability and consistency. Stable, settled and sane. For many people, this is the standard approach to life which has an apparent structure. Therefore, some people do not question what is given and follow what they are told.

However, the bad news is that common sense relies on the past and reluctantly accepts anything new, fresh, innovative. What does not comply with common sense is often labeled as foolish. Generally, it tends to be a conservative mindset. It defends from harmful practices, but does not stand well for exploration and novelty of things, ideas, opportunities. Innovation is far from common. Golden rule breathes wisdom. For something become wise it shall stand the test of time. The novelty is unwise, so that is why in the eyes of common sense it dies.

It is perfectly reasonable to have a guide in life. Common sense will stand for one. Commonsensical reality is practical. It does not require much mental energy to follow it. Also, it does not need thinking, just following the flag. It shows the way to go. Common practice brings common sense, so uncommon things are probably worst things to do. That is a rebuke before making any bold move against such flag. Would sound like mutiny against what is practically beneficial. Common sense is a good decision maker and problem solver until your mind reaches uncommon problems.

Someone may ask why anyone on this planet need to challenge something of such masterpiece like common sense? Questology is for progress and betterment, while common sense defends from mistakes and failure in your practical judgement. Two lines of potential development. Fulfilled with wisdom, logic, and science on which community agrees, common sense protects from misjudgements. Protective is often static while progress requires advancement and risk.

To question is to think. To think means to compute. Thinking habits compose the pensive quality. Questioning means thinking, so to think, compute, or question differ in subtleties despite being intimately connected. Questions delegate the mind to think, so your mind will follow questions or common sense. Questions initiate, common sense guards. Two flags to follow.

Moving forward, the mind thinks, calculates, projects and does a bunch of other stuff. To think is to compute. Computers and human mind run on logic which operates according to designed rules. The computer calculates according to logical rules as well as the mind uses logic to think. Files for computers are similar to thoughts. But computers get vulnerable if they catch viruses. The mind becomes vulnerable as well. Precisely that the mind, as well as any portable computer, can detect viruses which slow down the performance.

Computer viruses are real. Mental viruses are real as well, and the term was coined by Richard Dawkins - a militant British scientist who leisurely mocks religion for its dangerous effect. Viruses are biological, digital, mental as well as any other kind. Infections in mind mask themselves like little energy drainers. Sometimes they cause the conflict between personal perception and reality.

It is not necessarily religion that brings mental viruses. Religion might be a part of common sense in distinct communities. Any destructive or poisonous idea may convert into a harmful virus. Many would see no damage, but the mental health suffers. Poisoned or damaged body does not work. How do you think is the mind's health under poison or damage?

Noticing problems with the body is quick. Problems with the mind are more subtle. They are invisible, inaudible and untouchable because its mental. The way to realise them is to observe how they influence actions. Viruses in mind are too subtle to see. That is why the law of acuity does not go for accepting anything for real if reality has something to conceal.

Biological viruses are not spotted with the naked eye. As well as computer viruses are not found without special means. Mental viruses have an excellent shelter under prejudice. Then infected perception distorts from reality and creates a conflict because prejudice looks like reality, but is not. Such understanding might be a part of common sense in distinct communities making it imperfect and always questionable. The fastest way to spot prejudice is to ask yourself triple questions. Is anything in question is based on experience, natural science and number or reason? If the answer is no to all parts, there is more likely to have a virus smiling at your face.

Then, prejudice is the virus. Prejudice has no reason to support itself. No facts vote for it. Mental viruses sustain from your mental energy where you do nothing to prevent it. Needless to say that it harms the entire intelligent system. When prejudice comes into your mind, perception conflicts reality which is the dysfunction. That is where the mental architecture and its laws are the medicine.

Mental viruses make the government of thought unstable. Having one may sound nothing similar to evil. However, after seeing the impact of mental viruses, it is enough to look at physical and digital worlds. As your body is biotic, it is natural to have relationships with the natural world. Similarly, the digital environment - mind computes after all. Computer environment or web, they will deliver more than you expect.

From the digital perspective, computer viruses delete files, damage programs, and cause systems to crash. Your memory stores different elements of your personal experience. The way you think is like a program, so your attitude is like a system. Enough to see how mental viruses harm is to look at the analogy from the digital dimension. It is not always evident whether your computer has a virus or not. Equally, with the mind, it is not always evident if the mind has any infections. It starts making clear once it starts causing troubles due to misalignment with reality. Attitude problems are the signal for the dysfunction.

From the physical perspective, biological viruses multiply to harm or destroy the biological organism. Better not to test what smallpox, HIV or ebola viruses will do to your body. It is already well documented to spot the tragedy. Mental viruses are more subtle, but they also harm from the inside. Some are detrimental, some of them are plain prejudice to comfort people.

The mind is responsible for decisions someone makes. Just think what if radical religious belief, absolute political ideology or paranoia can do to the mind. In practice, there is a smaller scale of things that will impair decisions. Prejudice and self-delusion is the common one. In there, the question is the remedy from prejudice - remove the threat to the mental constitution.

The virus may, in fact, penetrate common sense. Even common sense can catch a virus. Radical religious conviction or political ideologies with the hostile elements in it will be like a spreading plague. Somewhere it is common sense - the part of tradition. You know perfectly what the indoctrination is. The brainwashed ones see such thing as common sense. Someone loses heads or are stoned to death for having a different opinion. It seems common for those executing such things. Such would be common sense. Or putting people in concentration camps was a common practice of the time. For a different mind, it is uncommon while for some minds it is very common. Common sense is not always so common.

You shall treat your mind like a basket of fresh fruits. It sounds impressive, but you shall mind fruits that are in the basket to prevent them from getting rotten. Otherwise, it may be some of the bananas, apples, oranges or else are already silently rotten. Not the best impact for the whole basket. Rotten fruits start affecting their surrounding putting all fruits in danger. The basket will decay very quickly.

Ideas in your head are like fruits in a basket, and you shall know what is in. In other words, to avoid putting rotten fruits into the basket first. This is an excellent analogy to display the first law of the mental architecture. To accept things for real only if they have nothing to conceal. If some harmful elements penetrate the mind, the infection, therefore, will make it blind.

Acuity involves skepticism to stay away from playful lures of first ideas. Ideas may get viral, and viruses do not look at themselves. The first impression may be misleading. No privilege has been granted to ideas - all of them are open to question. Mental viruses leave prejudice alone as if they were something right by default. With its aura of protection, it operates inside the mind. If you ever have seen negative, toxic or defeatist people, it might be because mental viruses ingrained in their attitudes influenced them. Such viruses are invisible, but even they have consequences. Then any action would get affected according to the nature of the virus which may cause misalignment with reality, denial or attitude problems.

Everyone may fall into prejudice easily and rapidly. When you come to the rule of acuity, you face the sharp edge instead. Prejudice will trap a vibrant mind in the cave with no light. So the law of acuity is to fight against prejudice, pierce and cut it. The law of acuity is sharp and skeptical - it does not always accept things at face value. It merely states that things you think are true might be wrong. No matter it is prejudice or false conviction, it is an unhealthy element. When you assume your admirable mind - the mental virus is like a mistake in the building. Like the building could collapse, so your mind is at risk.

Having an infected mind does not promise a very sharp outcome. This law penetrates things and acts from within. Mistakes in thinking are only the beginning. The excellent source for attitude issues. Those who think for a living, viruses will be as helpful as the illness for an athlete. If anything causes the grain of suspicion, the smart way is to question and to test it by yourself. Otherwise, your mind might become full of cats in no time. Misguided decisions, wishful or deluded thinking comes like prejudice in problem solving what will be stopping the advancement. Never accept anything for real if reality has something to conceal. That is to say about anything.

Coming to the rule of acuity, you face the sharp edge. The worst thing about logic - it is not democratic. Logic wears an autocratic mask. No compromises are made there for things are binary. Moreover, logic is selfish, so it cares for itself, not for people. Only intellectual standards democratise it to make it human. That is why you joined rationality with character. Rationality is autocratic - what is wrong does not live for long. Wrong facts, theories, and conclusions die - useless to apply in spite of their unlimited supply.

Moreover, logic shall shield the mind from rubbish and wrong matter. The worse than worst is when the rational mind accepts the deception for real. The mind computes what the thinking is. The law of acuity is like a microscopic view. It penetrates and focuses intensely on extracting the most basic useful elements. This law has apparent objects it works with. Everything coming as elements - information, knowledge or ideas are to consider. They might be obvious and silently deceptive. Being deceptive distorts the picture. The silent deception has no sound what puts your mind on the wispy ground. Something as substantial as smoke to build the mental palace for a joke.

The microscopic approach is what shatters the glass of delusion. The logic in quest applies the law of acuity to penetrate the facade of everything as to put something under the microscope. Then everything hidden gets visible. Deep focus finds its way into everything. The lens zooms things to the desired level to extract understanding of the simple. For digging deeper, questions add value by enforcing the law of acuity. It is capable of going from the macro to the micro level of understanding. You decide on aspects of practical use. A microscopic pierce approaches the useful elements. Acutely.

Even this book is complex at some point. What you hold is the book. It has its cover and pages where ideas are expressed in words. Words there are the most fundamental useful elements to convey ideas. To write a book, there is an act to manage complexity of ideas and put them into a comprehensible verbal form. Things move from simple elements - like words - into the complex one - like a book. Basics move to more advanced. In this case, this is the book, in other cases will be a computer, airplane or anything else.

Many are already familiar with such mental act. A simple visualisation takes a picture for example. You can zoom things in. Having digital photographs, you zoom certain parts to see things closer. Such action is very obvious. As you zoom photographs in and out, it is the process you can put everything on the mental microscope. Any problem is solved by penetrating into fundamentals and starting from there. The law of acuity has this purpose in its nature - to penetrate and stop at fundamentals which are simple and inherently right.

This is the vital part for problem solving. On the very fundamental level, the problem is its core plus complexity. If you do not understand something is because complexity messes up with your mind causing unnecessary confusion.

Simplicity + Complexity = Problem

You understand the simple, so you need to penetrate complexity to crack the problem. Everybody has problems, only problem's identity and intensity differ. This is a very simplistic version. There, complexity causes the trouble - something that one does not understand. Complexity is what may cover the matter with its entanglements, so the mind cannot see the obvious. For the resolution, the mind shall penetrate complexity until it comes clear enough to squeeze the solution. When solutions and understanding go on holiday, it is complexity that solved you. The law of acuity is the faculty to get your understanding back on track to eat problems like a snack.

Acuity is the sharp edge. It focuses on the problem rather than the solution because answers barely come before understanding the problem. So acuity intends to shatter the smoke of complexity to accelerate the solution. Instead of dealing with the smoke of complexity, the law of acuity targets the centre. Not symptoms, but the source.

To solve problems is to pierce into the centre of the problem and act from there. Think of a recent complex problem you untangled. The solution to the same problem would be more transparent now than it was dealing with it in the first time. Questions behave keenly and dig more in-depth than operate on the surface level. The law of acuity is the piercing through complexity which hides from you what is simple. The law of acuity invades the problem despite its immunity.

The Law of Division

*Divide each difficulty
into as many pieces as needed
for the problem to get defeated.*

Imagine you were given a task to transport an enormously colossal stone. From Brazil to England let's say. It is so dense that you neither can carry it nor ship because it will sink the ship. From the general perspective, such problem is too massive to solve it immediately. To take a stone with bare hands might be the standard way to solve problems somewhere. But it is not. It is not extremely helpful if the rock is of 15 tons. Instead what shall be done is an effort to split the stone into as many pieces as needed for the problem to get defeated. It divides a massive object - like any problem - into lightweight pieces which are approachable one by one.

So the law of division approaches complexity by piercing it firstly and dividing it secondly. Such is the elementary approach. The elementary approach makes things splittable like atoms from the inside out. Having a large stone to transport, means one sizeable splittable element. Divisions and subdivisions are the standard way to organise anything into smaller units. The elementary approach is what splits complicated things into simple ones. The gigantic stone visualises the abstract concept of problems. You cannot knock this down if you deal with the stone in the way it comes. The stone weights 15 tons. The stone is heavy, hard and unmovable. Problems may share the same qualities.

Having a problem of 15 tons - bare hands are not the solution. But if it becomes a multiplicity of 200 grams, it instead becomes lightweight and portable in your pockets. The question would be how to split it so accurately. For the thought experiment is a good number. Everyone here would agree that 200-gram rocks are slightly lighter than a monolith of 15 tons. To translate the analogy, you will notice that easy problems are done quickly because they are light, while complex ones demand more effort.

The central insight you will find is that simplicity seems to be lacking complexity. Problems are tricky because they are not simple - it has never been a secret. But the striking conclusion is that a severe problem is the grand amplification of simple ones. In other words - complexity is the amplified simplicity. That is why starting from basics is the clever beginning to tackle complex problems. So splitting anything into small elements translates difficulty into multiplicity. Essential details are in a composition of something advanced. Basic elements require less energy per engagement compared to the costly one. Splitting complexity solves it for it becomes too fragmented to threaten the mind.

Since there, every complexity has its gravity what makes it complicated. No matter what you take into a comparison. Everything has the core under the surface. Nucleus in the atom, CPU in the computer, the human heart under the skin, centre of the city, the government of the whole country, inner core of the planet and analogies go further. The critical aspect is to extract there what is useful - a concept of gravity behind things. It holds things together. A different shade of gravity Newton thought of. Gravity is the force what holds complexity alive.

To divide is the elementary approach. The law of acuity aimed at solving problems from the inside out. The law of division upgrades the effort. Every complexity has the base. Every organisation has the core. Every problem has its cause. Facing a problem, instead of combating with its surface, one penetrates the facade. Penetrating the problem is one way to approach its core to resolve.

Then the law of division puts it into as many pieces as needed for the problem to get defeated.

As you will see, elements can carry different nature. Physical, digital or mental - few to mention. They have their laws of operation. What we are concerned about belongs to the mental department which is also closely related to physical or digital ones. The physical dimension is why we took the example of a gigantic stone to introduce the law of division. Problems can be heavy like rocks. The same applies to concepts which are mental or information which tends to be digital. The law of the mental architecture seems to be applicable in more than one arena. Unfortunately, logic is invisible.

Splitting them sometimes is not enough. The elementary approach is like a tool of the chemist which analyses and then synthesises elements. Often there is the need to put them together in the more refined form. The law of division alone does not solve problems, but make the arrival of the solution significantly easier. It is clear when problems stop weighing 15 tons, but become a mountain of 200 grams pieces instead. Then picking up battles solves problems one by one. Both questions and answers are open for divisions to make them less complicated and more profitable instead. Answers are the currency for a problem solver.

The Law of Refinement

To form a functional design the only thing to do is to refine.

Not only you are rewarded with talents. The world has its own, so it puts you in the sea of complexity. The world exercises its talents while you are invited to pay back in return with yours. As you already know, problems and decisions are full of complication and uncertainty. The world is a troubling place for someone. It is not always working smoothly, so some cases promise a challenge. Like the large stone, you faced as a thought experiment. Despite your mind cracks the rock into as many pieces as needed for the problem to get defeated, it is not everything done to resolve the issue.

To remove or reduce complexity from the task, the law of refinement is the exercise. It eliminates the irrelevance from the equation and cleans the clutter. Previously, the mind zoomed into the issues or deconstructed them for the decisive finals. Then, the law of refinement is for a go. Imagine, the example as weighty as 15 tons rock. Once it gets deconstructed, there are many smaller pieces which still weight 15 tons if combined. The question is whether or not all of them are needed to get transported. If it is for scientific research, a small fraction would be more than enough to keep geologists busy. So you do not need to tackle the whole stone.

There is always the standard to deal with the deconstruction. Refinement follows the guideline. In fact, what makes problems difficult is entanglement in their intricate nature. Things you need or want to understand but do not - that is the problem. This often happens due to complexity. So the law of refinement is the way to untangle entanglements to remove the unwanted complexity. Problems are not simple. That is why things are to be called problems in the first place. When they get split into as many pieces as needed to get them defeated there is the refining principle to achieve the real victory.

In decision making, when you have to choose, and you have many choices, but you cannot finalise, you have trouble. Some will relate to such situation. The developed world offers the abundance which naturally inspires the pain of choosing. Typically, when the solution overwhelms someone in charge, then a taxing effect will follow next. For instance, picking dinner out of 123 options in a new restaurant will be overwhelming if all of the choices are more than satisfactory. The absence of the standard makes the situation awkward. Everywhere, the abundance of alternatives eventually makes decisions hard compared to one with fewer options. The law of refinement is there to cut some things out. There must be the standard which decides the relevance of ideas. It decides, so the irrelevant goes out.

Regardless of the area, complexity comes in dilemmas, trilemmas or whatemmas. It is the decision to pick something out. In practice, it is easy to choose something having only two or three alternatives. Obviously, harder when they multiply to 20 or 30. Or when it comes to data science - it will get thousands and million elements to refine - you write computer programs to deal with data to make decisions for you. Coming on the practical stage, the standard in the person becomes like an algorithm in the computer. Either it is 2, 20 or 2000 elements the principle goes the same - it removes misaligning elements what makes the decision easier. Your priority is the authority. The rule of refinement is all about shaving things out according to the standard.

What makes decisions difficult is the number of alternatives to choose from. Paralysis in decision making is a common reason why many of them get postponed. The paradox of choice is a well-known phenomenon. Barry Schwartz - American psychologist -

delivered a brilliant TED talk about it. Opportunities cripple the decision making, so one stops doing anything. Having the abundance of choices navigates to paralysis rather than liberation. Opportunities paradoxically make the mind challenged enough to decide. Then too many alternatives are the problem for making a final decision. The doubt will provide the devastating escort service to make you nervous.

In fact, freedom is the fundamental value. Following the paradox of choice, it is the number of choices shall be leading to liberation. Naturally, the higher the potential of choice - the fewer restrictions. That is the "official dogma" to maximise welfare as he calls it. The increased number of options quickly invites the paradox. That is where liberation invites paralysis. Increased alternatives grow the difficulty like a plant. There are too many things to compare and regret the decision after.

Abundance is another name for the state of many choices. High numbers of alternatives make a choice difficult. Having such whatemma is the substantial reason for procrastination. The athletic decision making greets disability rather than agility. In choosing things, nobody wants to regret which quickly enters the stage. For example, in among 123 choices, picking one instantly gets it compared to 122. There is regret in the ambush. The intent for freedom by increasing alternatives is potential servitude to ambivalence. Smells problematical as the choice will be not good enough compared to what is left unchosen.

The more options, the easier to regret. Such is the typical consequence while having no standard to align alternatives accordingly. Opportunity cost implies that you need to sacrifice something to get anything. Naturally, people do not like sacrificing things. Principles are not human, but decisions are unavoidable. Losing less is progress. Then refinement perhaps is the straighter way to liberation than the abundance of choice. It involves the standard based on priority. The priority is the authority. So it aligns things around its pulling gravity. What does not fit goes out of orbit. Such loss is a winning strategy with its cost. Standards get set.

Having a multiplicity of choices and agreeing on every opportunity lubricate the moment, but distracts from the primary objective. It leaves less mental energy to what is essential. Distraction is a compelling state to limit the advancement in its hesitation. Turning green light to everything often leaves very little time to execute on all things properly.

Therefore, the law of refinement cuts things out if they do not align with the standard. The standard filters the world of information and opportunities. When someone is a vegetarian, one does not eat meat, so it quickly drops the irrelevant choices in the restaurant. Then, when it comes to decision making, the law of refinement reduce the level of options by simply cutting irrelevant ones out.

More is less. That is why the law of refinement shaves off unfitting alternatives according to the standard to bring more value. If you asked what standard, the answer is yours. The law of refinement prioritises information and removes the clutter according to your design. Experience and questions form the standard. Eventually, when there is a personal standard, many of the alternatives are getting out of frame. This is a brilliant achievement for a decision maker. Many things are found irrelevant and so removed from the current equation. What you need is to accept or design the standard.

Then such outlook dramatically improves decision making as choices are removed from the frame considerably. Refinement fights competently against abundance which votes for complexity to get an office in your mind. The higher the standard, the lower the supply of options. That is why someone with lowered standards has the higher input of alternatives what may cause unnecessary confusion. When you eliminate all elements except remaining under the pressure of refining law, even the most unwanted and the most unconvincing elements are the least wrong, therefore the truest and healthy thing to do. Refining law shaves the weak alternatives and survival of the fittest option prevails.

People are guided by specific reasons to do one thing or another. It sets up the standard automatically. Then people make and take decisions based on that. In theory, if there is no standard, so then there is no focus. When there is no focus, then it is vague what is fitting and what is not. Then it becomes a little bit tricky to shave the irrelevant because there is also nothing relevant. To know what is important to you, you need to set your standard. To see the standard, you need to know the answer. To see the answer, you need to ask your questions.

If there is a struggle to establish what is important, then the law of refinement cannot distinguish what fits and what does not. Nobody goes far if no decision is made - only stands in front of whatemmas. It is hard to decide if there is not something for. That is why the standard matters. It becomes better defined and refined if you ask your questions. And so the practical benefit coming from the standard is its support in decision making and holding focus against complexity.

However, the practice offers a more straightforward picture. Many have their needs, wants and various preferences. So there is already the standard to put a base for decisions. For example, if people want to be content, most likely they will not do intentionally what makes them discontented - the path is clear - to happiness. Alternatives not leading there are removed out. Or a sweeter example. If someone loves macarons, it enforces the standard to pick one once a person enters the bakery. Standards are definable what shows decisions instead of leaving someone in the paradox of choice.

Then minimising choices is the optimal and athletic decision making. Knowing what not to do tells clearly what shall be done. Refinement is the powerful approach to decision making. Then, when any dilemma, trilemma or whatemma come, the standard prioritises and decides. Many would know Warren Buffet - American investor and philanthropist. His approach to decision making embodies the law of refinement. Dressed in different cloth though. He is a figure for his wealth and wisdom. The Internet has many stories to tell about 5/25 decision making rule.

Perhaps that is the finalising act to design your tactics where whatemma suck you in. The 5/25 decision making rule is relatively simple. The whole story goes like this. A person came to Warren Buffet to ask for guidance on what one needs to do in one's life. Buffet asked the person to write 25 things down one would like to do, and the person succeeded in making a list. Then, Warren Buffet continued. After 25 elements were written, he instructed to pick five of those out and ignore those 20 unselected. Such thing was done. The unselected were shaved out, so the mind became saved from unnecessary complexity. Complexity was refined and the standard set. The person left having five alternatives in the end. The priority is your authority.

A progressive step in making a choice. The message seems to be intuitive. Assume that you have 100% of energy to devote for things. Then, for a comparison, if you stick with 25 important things, you would spend 4% of your energy to each of them. It is a tiny number of energy and if you like equality. If you do not, you will devote your energy chaotically causing even more confusion in the end. Also, it is a constant jumping from one option to another. A confused mind is one of the potential consequences. It is a poorly managed situation compared to what may come after refining options.

On the other hand, cutting 20 elements out and staying with five, in the end, brings a higher chance to win. Consequently, they are the most important ones for you. Otherwise, you would not be left with them. So what is unique about focus and staying with five elements instead of 25? The advantage comes in spending energy on things of greater importance. For a similar demonstration, five things will require 20% of energy each. It is an almost invisible increase of contribution - just by 500% compared to the jumping around 25 options. We must agree that in life there is more than one decision to be made. It is not about following a concrete model - like Warren Buffet's. More about of logical faculty which embraces the refining principle to shave unfitting things off.

The law of refinement, instead of deconstructing things, it shaves them out. Not everything, only the irrelevant. After all, it is not enough to split any complexity into as many pieces as needed for the problem to be defeated. Imagine, you divide - then what? Conceptually, having many tiny elements eventually organises them better. In fact, the law of refinement has few very straightforward guidelines. Relevance and simplicity are what matters. The bombardment of information are carriers of complexity. Simplicity is leading the way. The fewer choices, the more comfortable for the mind to exercise deep focus. The mind prioritises things - the unimportant goes out. One aspect of the function in decision making.

In the end, this is the standard to determine the excellence, not the comparison to existing options. Knowing the standard, imagine two situations. Starting with 123 dishes to pick for dinner. Having no standard will lead you to compare option with option. But if it happens you have the standard, irrelevant alternatives go out of game almost immediately. Options get compared to the standard, not other options. If options are not good enough to satisfy the standard, they get out. The potential for confusion gets minimal.

In the decision making, there must be the standard. Otherwise, the abundance is leading to servitude to ambivalence rather than liberation. With no standard, to consider every option is mentally costly. Also, not very effective on a daily basis where abundance circulates. Standards create the loop of excellence. However, making decisions with no rules eventually forms the standard. That is why bad choices often improve their quality. Poor choices are an excellent learning opportunity. Costly in its nature, but the merit shall be coming later.

The question is an excellent initiator to determine the relevance. Elimination may make the law of refinement slightly judgy. It was about the decision making part - you tame complexity by refining it. The abundance of choice is the primary force stopping someone from making decisions. In problem solving, there are other redundant elements. Problems and decisions are inevitable, but the refining principle tackles them both.

In problem solving, there are no alternatives as they are common in decision making. There is a replacement of complexity - it gains another identity. Not options what matters there, but complications to shave them out. In contrast, a particular problem is singular what invites to focus more on complications rather than work on quantity. There is another form of abundance - density. The intricacy of things in products, processes or concepts. Rather than expanding in quantity, it spreads in density. Problems are difficult because they are dense.

A problem is a singular unit. Despite being singular, they are complex. Combined having many unique units integrated into them. A process may have multiple steps and guidelines. A product may have thousand individual pieces composing it. However, it hides its intricate complication behind the surface of the single dense element. The refining principle there is to remove excessive components from the system without harming its performance. Not alternatives there are in question. Problems for sure will be extensive regarding elements they contain within. For example, if a single product has been made using 1000 unique pieces. Ability to retain the identical performance of the same product with 800 pieces makes the product refined so less dense, but equally complicated.

The law of refinement is like shaving. The shaver is the ideal example, is not it? Like the face gets cleaned up, so ideas, products or services will receive similar treatment. It is greater to achieve the simplicity of the complex than complexity of the simple. Everybody will complicate a trivial matter, but not everybody will manage complexity to make it look simple. For the practical ends, simpler things are more desired. That is why refining principle is at place. Just wonder which equation you would pick. For the sake of complex over simple preference, take a clear mathematical example:

$$(1 - (4 \times 2) + 3 - 6/3 + 7) + 1 = 6/2 - 8/4 + 1$$

And

$$1 + 1 = 2$$

Both means the same. Regardless of preferences, the second expression is much more straightforward. While preferences are not absolute, many would pick the second line for the practical use. For understanding, communication, and application. For some people, the first one may look more exciting manipulation of numbers. For the useful purpose, the second is optimal. Some problems may seem like the first equation until your understanding makes them look like the second.

The reason why mathematics is the example there is because you cannot escape from the number. It is the fundamental component found everywhere. You will discover mathematics in economics. You will find mathematics in architecture. And you will taste mathematics in physics. Is there anything that would not contain mathematical elements? Facts and figures are the hardcore details. Things are expressed in numbers - space in cubic meters, territory in square meters, length in meters, etc. It is almost impossible to escape from the number. Even if you tried so, you would use your two legs running at speed x miles per hour.

Look from another perspective. Manufacturing is the process of production by using machinery. The solution is the product. Logic is the machinery there. If you heard lean thinking term, the law of refinement is behind it. Lean thinking is the business methodology to organise human activity to deliver more benefits to the society. The way how it is done is by eliminating waste. Some elements are bringing unwanted sophistication which is neither profitable nor particularly helpful. As you will witness, the law of refinement itself has a particular benefit in business management where waste is the target for shaving it out. Reducing the redundancy increases effectiveness. The logic in quest gets into business to exercise its fitness.

What about lean manufacturing? There is another lean model applied particularly in production. Lean manufacturing is collecting business practices and methods to eliminate waste. The same topic is there. Elimination of waste is the practical result of the law of refinement which dared to be logical. Intelligent faculty eventually eliminates waste and increase efficiency with less complication. Reducing waste reduces the cost. The logic in quest enters into production to serve more than a plain deduction.

Think about lean product development. There are many services with complications. The lean way removes the excess by cutting off waste. For example, extra processes, unwanted features, and defects are something wasteful. For example, you have a product with 1000 unique combining elements. If you can guarantee the same functionality and quality with 800 individual pieces, so density will get simplified. To refine and make redundancy extinct is welcome in lean development. Reducing the redundancy increases the processing speed. The logic in quest enters into product development to make it elegant.

What all three examples have in common is waste. Waste make things complicated. Even useless things are costly. Lean of everything operates in the refining principle. Coming back to the mind, when waste is removed from there, decisions are taken athletically, and problems approached with agility. You are more likely to remove the obesity from the mind to keep it lean.

Laws of the mental architecture are not left only for concepts and ideas, but faces the real world. Intelligent faculty combines principles to be applied into practice. Unfortunately, they are invisible, but remain sensible. Logic employs its deduction to push basics forward by invisible instruction.

Chapter 6:
The Third Principle of Questology:
The Logic in Quest

"*Pure logic is the ruin of the spirit.*"
Antoine de Saint-Exupéry

"*The important thing is not to stop questioning. Curiosity has its own reason for existing.*"
Albert Einstein

"*If you do not know where you are going, any road will take you there.*"
Lewis Carroll

The mental architecture has at least three laws which will operate regardless of the nature of the problem. They apply to physical, mental and digital worlds similarly. Only the quality of the element will differ. A stone, a thought of a stone or a hologram of a stone cover three dimensions. It must be quite exciting to notice disinterest shown by the mental architecture. On all three dimensions, laws will operate similarly - only the type of things will change.

Next, this principle of questology embraces a different tone slightly. Looking at what already happened in the book, the first principle expressed the inevitable link between the question and the answer. Then, the second principle designed the mental architecture to inspect everything that may look like the answer - information, ideas, knowledge, etc. The third principle is the logic in quest which finds its structural foundation in the mental architecture. Like an upgrade. Logic there is the baseline to form questions, and the question has its logic behind.

Questology is the vibrant way to unlock the potential of the mind. Without questions, questology has no right to be called this way. It has no rights at all. It is a mental model, a tool to initiate your mind. The fork assists in dining while questology assists the mind to solve problems and make decisions, invent and discover. To question is to think. Thinking requires some rules and should not be confused with dreaming or active imagining. So questions gain their logical structure from the mental architecture. One part of support is logic, another one - your intentions. Individuals ask questions, so intent is in it by default.

Having a structure is equally important as being flexible. The structure defines, flexibility expands. Like the conventional compass. It has its directions defined in 360 degrees. The mental architecture is the structure you put into a compass. The first principle already set-up a connection, now it is the logic in quest to finalise it. Logic is invisible and organisational as well as is grammar. Grammar seems to be vital to form a question. They are not destined to be boring - they will start in style when you put things into a logical structure.

The logic in quest combines the athletic question put on the structure. Moving forward, this is the third principle to join two key elements there. One is ability, and another one is utility. Quite interestingly questions create opportunities, but at the same time, there is a restrictive force that follows.

Logic is circular, to stretch out structural boundaries it needs the force. Logic limits and structures the input. Without limitations, questions will grow like uncontrollable Twitter's feed. Ability to pose questions may be excessive giving answers you do not need to make you overthinking or distracted. More valuable are quality answers they deliver. That is where you need the standard.

Questions, first, get their ability to initiate answers, but the standard, secondly, decides on utility. So this part of questology is about those two elements.

The fitness there depends on how well questions perform. The flair to pose a question in the air is ability to question things. That is to say about the logic in quest. But this is not all. Beside this, there are other metrics to measure whether some questions need to be asked or not. The logic in quest brings simple design to question things expansively. Too many questions inspire for many answers - a direct road to overstimulation. Not all of them are equally important what would take time to regard them all. Askability score is the restrictive force to drive individual questions. Utility is there to invest in ability.

Questions are not for themselves, so knowing how to put them is only a part of the story. For the question to work, it needs to have its performance. Questions are elastic, so their increase your fitness of the mind. The analogy of fitness is an excellent way to embody the versatility. Anyone can make a question in the interview, in the workshop or the workplace. Communication of any kind gets upgraded due to questions fuelling the flaming fire. Questions are like vitamins to start something on. They bring new insights to consider. The problem is that even having a question in your head may be hard to verbalise it. Then the focus goes on a patterned ability first.

Questions delegate and lead your mind - the brand new function and fitness of progress. They are functional. The mental architecture alone makes the whole thing this way. To approach answers and everything of this kind, your ability is the skill in the making. To make question fitting, it is about knowing the context around. The logic in quest is the mode and flair to pose a question in the air. It is about functionality to meet its standards - askability score. It decides if questions are fitting. For the optimal performance of questions, someone like you would succeed drastically in knowing what questions to ask.

Askability scores up its metrics aligning with your motives and intentions. This is the standard to decide over questions. Unfortunately, such is the limiting force for your betterment. The judgy standard to approach intended questions to limit infinite supply according to what is needed than what it is possible. It draws a fine line between a possibility and the need. The society does not need every possibility at the moment, but a good question makes every need possible. Needs are more practical than possibilities. Ability to extend the possibility and satisfy the need.

Triadic Style
The Function and Ability

> *"Judge a man by his questions rather than his answers."*
> **Voltaire**

You start building questions after you polish your mental architecture. The structure there becomes the backbone. Triadic style is certain acrobatics to mobilise your mind. Questions do act for the vitality and for answers, do not they? Knowing the question-answer bond and the mental architecture, the style builds up on the top accordingly. Triadic style is the pattern to employ three types of questions. This is the space to convert questions to an entirely new level.

In general, complex problems and tough decisions are not fun things to do, but they are inevitable. That may be the reason why someone may run away from problems or jump into the indecisiveness' bandwagon. Like any skill, questioning tackles the inevitable. Questioning fuels old patterns with new ideas and drag them forward. Questioning shall be the unique style of mind to fight apathy and boredom. Questions delegate the mind to a dynamic approach, so it becomes active and rescued from passivity.

Triadic style perfectly serves to explore things up. As you will see, questions are various - they bring multiple answers. There, everyone will find out things according to their liking. It is evident that questioning is the starting point. The most important thing is how to question in style. The style is the flair to pose the question in the air. As you heard continuously repeated, it is for problem solving and decision making. Every problem and every decision is taken significantly quicker if first of all someone pays attention to:

Defining things
Explaining how things work
Finding the reason and purpose of things

It is pretty straightforward. Basics give the context and strength. Firstly, the definition provides a reliable target to think of. Missing to see the problem makes it invisible. So defining the problem is the starting point to crack it. Additionally, the definition makes things comprehensible. Seeing no problem leads to no solution. Metaphorically, you cannot fix the car if there is no car broken in front of you. Equally, with any challenge, it must be a defined issue in front of your eyes. Defining problems and things, in general, makes them visible. When things get visible, everyone will assault issues with devoted concentration. Definitions define problems, so they are started to be solved.

How about explanations? The second part of triadic style. Things are more than of a definition. Various things work having complex systems within. So the clear understanding of the function is the starting point to solve a problem. Previously, complications and entanglements happened because definition and functionality remained unclear. For example, to build an airplane, one needs to know how it works - the order in which combining materials are joined. Or, having health problems, and curing them people pay a visit to a doctor who knows how the human body works. Knowledge of how brings a certain advantage in solving problems. The question is leading there.

Finally, finding the reason behind things is the third element. For example, if you throw keys vertically, they will fall and make noise. For this basic example, you will see that keys have dropped down because they were thrown up. The causality is what matters there. The question of why is the strongest appeal to reason. It is not enough to catch definitions and explanations of how things work. Knowing why things happen in the way they do is the beginning to approach problems from within. If there is the problem, something did not work out. The problem is the consequence of the previous action, so knowing the reason is the starting point to solve it out.

Three parts combine triadic style. Definitions, explanations, and reasons are the targets. The question-answer bridge is the example that mastering questions will lead to answers sooner or later. Triadic style equates to the skill for making questions. First of all, it starts as a flexible expression of the intentional mind. What does it mean? When you want something, you ask a question to get the answer. There your intention appears. Otherwise, you would not be asking questions. Then this is a natural expression of curiosity which you put into the structure.

You use mental structures when you think. Background and knowledge influence your attitude. Logic there is apparent. Once logic becomes clear how to put your intention into a framework, it works like the engine. Everybody can personalise grammar and structure intentions while initially, grammar is impersonal, and the intention is structureless. Grammar is the structure that gives the rational framework for the question. Everything else is left for the intention. That is where the alliance between character and rationality manifests in its verbal form. The verbal is the tip of the iceberg - the mental architecture is underwater. The line between mental and verbal looks like this. The mental structure is metallic. Your speech is customised.

At this moment, thinking is less evident than speaking, so you expose language more than the mental architecture. Verbalised thoughts are more visible than ideas alone. You do not see logic, but you hear and see questions. To question is to think. In the verbal context, once words are put in the flow, they direct towards something. Then, the question is the perfect reflection of the intention. So questions make thoughts and intentions more visible. The mental architecture is unseen.

When it comes to questions, you will find a verbal structure behind them. Structures are patterns to govern intentions - questions get framed. Intentions are individual which shall not be discussed here. Because what fits for John may not fit for George and vice versa, but if both are interested in something they will use similar structures about different things. The structure gives the pattern and ability. Questioning is the skill.

Patterns are crucial there. Only questions may slightly differ, but the structure will remain. They are easy to notice. Questions have their grammatical constitution. When it comes to asking about places "where?" Is often involved. If you ask about time then "when?" Is the bright start. Knowing this, you step one step forward where the majority of questions settle into three categories:

What? - Questions of definition. Hunts for clarity.
How? - Questions of explanation. Pursues functionality.
Why? - Questions of purpose. Searches for reason.

That is the pattern for triadic style. Everybody knows the structure, so the benefit comes with employment. The moment to realise that questions are the expression of the skill. They strive for answers as other skills are used for their applicable reasons. You know that mastery of a skill develops a pattern. Reading, writing, speaking - are some skills. Counting, planning, managing - just of another kind. In there you find a specific logic that binds the entire thing together - it follows logic of the consistent flow. What matters is the pattern, the habit of thinking. To master the mode of asking questions is patterned, the intention is loose.

Triadic style is the way to target the vague, convoluted and aimless to solve them out. Unclear things get defined to get solved. Complicated things become explained to get answered. Unreasonable things are unfolded to get solved. All of those things in one way or another approach the level where the original intention takes place. Problems or decisions are not left for themselves. To solve a problem is like flexing muscles. Enough effort brings complexity down. The question is an excellent starter where triadic style delegates your mind to think and find out what matters the most. Triadic style finds its support in logical structure until it becomes a natural part of your life. It is the mode of mind which always asks why - one of the three ways you will apply.

On the very fundamental level, if you can manage x, y, and z - you get the pattern, so you can manage everything. For example, managing a bank, hotel or a restaurant are different forms of management. It is management after all. The same skill is applied in distinct contexts. The difference involves some subtleties, but the management remains. Reading novels, biographies or news is still reading. Counting money, stars or cars is counting as well. Skills are patterned. For baking questions, patterns apply. The thing of highest importance is to establish the pattern to pose questions.

Moreover, decisions based on data are superior to conclusions based on nothing. The pattern for questioning is structural. It is clear to see that repeating particular things over and over again eventually develops consistency and discipline. This is skill related. It forms a pattern which will represent the skeletal nature of the whole thing. Skills arise from patterns. Structure alone is impractical. The pattern becomes the skill once it gets applied in practice. That is why it needs to make abundantly clear that patterns are the skeleton for the further dressing up.

That is why going in triadic style you need grammar to navigate intentional questions. Questions are a natural part of the language. You already know that logic governs thoughts in your mind. Grammar is structural as well. Consequently, grammar will be the structure for communication. For example, American linguist Noam Chomsky proposed a concept of universal grammar. Such structure plays its part in the language. A good starting point to find out the balance. It is clear that behind every language you will find some patterns. As well as behind every question you will see some logic and intention.

Then going in triadic style and using grammar for questions are becoming the restrictive force for creativity. You get the structure from the mental architecture. In other words, it is logic. It is gravity holding experiences, knowledge and other mental things together - like a skeleton holds muscles. The skeleton is frozen, and muscles are mobilising. What a distinction. The skeleton creates the gravity for the functionality. To operate on the pattern, the skeleton there is the case - logic is the skeleton. Regarding questology, for going to fitness and utility, you start with the function and ability. Logic is the intelligent start; speech is a linguistic one.

The mental architecture is the invisible logic. For the analogy, take the human standard as an example. You do not see your bones directly. They are covered in muscles and skin. Such is the starting point. Logic is the skeleton, and muscles are the mobilising force of the body. Backgrounds, education, knowledge, experience, and memorable things form the internal content to stand for muscles in this context - they mobilise the whole body and gives it a direction. Muscles to the skeleton are like the verbal to mental. The verbal aspect is being put on the mental architecture like muscles place bones.

From there you will reveal the metaphor holding things together. As the mental architecture and logic become exposed as a vital part of question making, there are other steps to fulfil the matter. Logic is the skeleton which is not enough for the complete realisation of things. You have joined rationality with character for that purpose. It plays perfectly in the metaphor of human layers.

The skeleton and muscles form a skeletal muscle. Naturally, muscles always cover bones and the skeleton hold muscles. Otherwise, someone would be lifeless if those two things were separate. This analogy is applied to the mind as well. Muscles bring fitness to the body, and words bring fitness to grammar.

Then, knowledge and understanding perfectly represent the mobilising force. People do and speak things because they have a grasp. Words are to make thoughts visible. It matters in asking questions to oneself and others. A verbal element is a perfect outfit. Both private or public questions can be verbalised. Directly or indirectly. This is where verbal ability operates with agility. Eventually, the flair to pose questions in the air witness something expressive. Language is the element to employ. While grammar brings the function, words mobilise the performance.

However, to ask a question to expand your knowledge you shall know something. Otherwise, there is nothing to be developed or improved. It implies the first knowledge and the further derivation of it. Knowledge is like muscles - flexing it brings the improvement and accumulation. Muscles energise the entire organisation what increases fitness levels. Muscles give movement to the body, while the skeleton maintains stability. To verbalise the mind and make logic useful, the person goes with the logic in quest.

Then, language plays a significant role in asking questions. The mind gets verbal to acquire a visible form. The truth is simple - grammar is automatic, as the skill. Once learnt it gets applied quickly. The real impact comes since it deals with everyday situations. Questions delegate your mind to speed up thinking to disrupt the familiar gravity of thought and action. To question is to think, act and create, so answers become thoughtful, actionable and creative. The structure limits imagination, but defines the undefinable and explains the unexplainable. Such skeleton is the limitation and the foundation to build a question on. The skeleton is motionless where muscles develop to improve ability. Knowledge fulfils the frame.

Triadic style gets into the playground as a skill which has its structure as well as content. To solve problems and make decisions, you will apply a particular mental model with its unique design. A metallic framework of logic to open up the horizon for adventures where unseen can be seen.

As you know, the first element deals with definition questions which seek clarity. A practical demonstration where you will apply structure and intent in triadic style. The part of triadic style and random examples following the pattern:

-What is a plan?
-What is it to create and manage a company?
-What is the image of a better person?
-What is survival?
-What is an excellent piece of art?
-What does it mean to listen to pleasant music?
-What is happiness?

-What is an excellent book?
-What is creativity?
-What is a keen perception after all?
-What is productivity?
-What is a weight loss?
-What is the concept of human nature?
-What is a problem?
-What does it mean to have life clear?
-What are five finely selected countries to visit a year?
-What is the size of income after a 15% increase?
-What is an exotic language?
-What is a card trick?
-What is perfect dinner to you?
-What is it?
-What…?

Such list delegates your mind to think and define things. Every question above is different in their intentions, but have the same structure. You have noticed something repetitive. In this part, going in triadic style starts with "what?". It gives a perfect target for the mind to strike and extract the definition. To structure the unstructured. Or if you like, bring order to the chaos. Boundaries are good. The absence of them draws no separation between one thing and another. Nobody is protected from falling into a fog of ambiguity where the smoke of confusion may blind you. To beat this vague situation, defining questions bring clarity.

Some questions are simple, some of them are sophisticated. It does not replace the fact that defining questions bring a better understanding of what is what. Confusion is not something desired. Clarity is often much more preferred. Everyone will develop a better judgement if they can form a definite thing to be judged. Prerequisite for this is understanding of things. When the question assists in finding definitions of the unknown - it prevents from falling into a mental fog. The pattern is already exposed, practice is what left to be made.

Sometimes knowing what is what is not enough to arrive at the decision or solve the problem. The style of the vibrant mind does not come solely from one source. The definition provides a surface of the thing without digging deeper. The world is more than a definition. So there is a natural extension - explanations of things. Wording talks for itself. In this way, the question leads your mind to figure out how things work not only of what they are. The second dimension of understanding. Questions of how will direct the mind to find out how things - like computers, airplanes or whatever - work if this is the intention. Or processes like production or communication. Or ideas like capitalism or democracy. It is the fundamental understanding of how. It begins the expansion of the practical knowledge of things around.

Going forward, someone may know what is what. The problem may appear on how to create such thing. For example, talking about a product, service or idea. Many will define their products, services or ideas outstandingly. Even while starting out. The real struggle is to get to know how to build or understand them and their working. And by going in triadic style, you will create massive lists of potential questions according to the pattern. With a single change in the structure, you replace one element and set a different tone. Explanation questions are questions of how in the patterned list as follows:

- How to make a plan?
- How to create and manage a company?
- How to be a better person?
- How to survive?
- How to create a piece of art?
- How to compose music?
- How to be happy?
- How to write a good book?
- How to be more creative?
- How to be more perceptive?
- How to be more productive?
- How to lose weight?
- How to understand human nature?
- How to solve a problem?
- How to make your life clear?
- How to visit five countries in a year?
- How to increase personal income by 15%?
- How to learn an exotic language in a year?

-How to master a card trick?
-How to cook perfect dinner today?
-How to expand this list?
-How....?

There are plenty of questions with their requests for the mind to move forward. Only answers are left to be found. Many lines in the list may be irrelevant, but the pattern is more important than the list of questions. Mastering the pattern makes questioning natural. Mastering lists recreate them from memory. Patterns are the elegant replacement for lists. But for the patterns to form, derive them from the repeating lists. Lists hide patterns.

Questions of how are considered to be important elements of understanding. It is second to questions of why. Consequently, the last component of triadic style summons reasoning. This type of questions the most difficult to find answers to. Deep thinking is for figuring out the connection between the reason and the result. This is the mode of thought which requires the most energy because profound questions are more than a cheerful walk in the park.

Questions of why often gain the most of the attention. The movement to Start With Why is getting huge traction in the English speaking world. Initiated by Simon Sinek - celebrated American author and public speaker. On the individual level, they bring the sense of purpose for people to live fulfilled lives. Instead of doing things that drain human potential, knowing your why initiates to the personal fulfilment. It is a powerful force to mobilise individuals to follow their passions. Then, Simon Sinek encourages to Start With Why and none of the ways round. Quantitively, more people know what they do than those who understand why they do so. Then, Starting With Why makes you unique because many do not do it.

Starting With Why is an inspiring way to live the life. Starting With Why is one thing which is useful for many people. When everyone finds out the work where efforts are meaningful and bring more value than take energy, then fulfilment is the likely outcome. However, the problem with it is that not everyone knows how to start this way. It serves more like a slogan and advice. More practical is knowledge of how to Start With Why. In this context, the explanation would be more practical, but practical things rarely inspire. Knowing the method how to start is practical. More important than Starting With Why is to begin with a relevant question every time.

The final part of triadic style is there. What differs is the mode you design questions. Having a definition and explanation, it lacks profundity. Questions of why give the reason or purpose depending on how you design it. Take a quick glide to squeeze the pattern:

- **Why** should someone create a plan?
- **Why** does someone need to manage a company?
- **Why** do we need to be better people?

-Why do we need to survive?

-Why is art important?

-Why is music pleasant?

-Why is happiness the goal?

-Why does a person need to write a good book?

-Why is creativity the source of creation?

-Why are perceptive individuals better learners?

-Why is productivity the reason for excellent results?

-Why do people care to lose weight?

-Why do people wish to understand themselves?

-Why do problems need to be solved?

-Why do people wish to live clear life?

-Why do you want to visit only five countries a year?

-Why the increase in income matters?

-Why do we need to learn languages?

-Why card tricks matter?

-Why do you need to eat dinner?

-Why do we need to expand this list?

-Why...?

Why Starting With Why is a good idea? More critical is to begin with a relevant question every time - questions of why are in the territory of the logic in quest. Questology first and foremost is for setting up questions according to the need. You already met the importance of the pattern. Questions of what and how have a repetitive design to grasp triadic style. When it comes to questions of why, people can bake them equally on thin air. Because they can. The patterns are presented. Questioning is patterned. Intentional and intelligent, so less random. Probably Starting With Why means mastering the compass of the mind. Then such triadic style contains three modes of questioning. Each has its targets, each has its functions, and each fits for specific occasions:

The question of what - defines directly
The question of how - explains elegantly
The question of why - thinks thoughtfully

Going in triadic style is relevant everywhere - the force of the mental compass. You know planes are designed to fly; submarines are for deep waters. But then it would be bizarre if submarines would fit everywhere. The attempt to do anything different than it was designed for will make someone to wake up. Questology as a compass is of a different kind with similar elements in it - it is designed to solve problems, make decisions and lead the mind with questions. That is to say about functionality. Also - some things are universal, so questology fits them.

The structure based on grammar fits everywhere where the language and thought apply. The structure is more fitting than the particular question. That is to say that triadic style is applicable pretty much everywhere because of the pattern. Business - what, how, why? Personal life - what, how, why? Social life - what, how, why? Professional life - what, how, why? No matter what dimension of life you will take for your example, it will remain stable like grammar builds the gravity for the language.

The question of why is indeed interesting because it applies on two fronts. In Starting With Why tone, it seems to be setting the purpose in front. When you know why you do what you do, it brings you a clear direction of something to move forward. It must be an inspiring moment. The question of why connects with the purpose which is in the future. When you assume that people know why they do what they do, it may say that they see the future which inspires them to move to it. The optimistic approach connects with the future and inspires for it, but it often does not solve problems. Questions of how perhaps instead should be jumping over problems like athletes jump over barriers in the steeplechase.

However, questions of why have another mode of acting. They, in fact, are questions to accelerate problem solving. It sounds amusing - inspiration connects with problem solving as if triadic style has been evolving. Two in one. Let's meet another side of the medal. You already heard the causality hidden beneath. Questions of why do not target the future only. It reflects the problematic aspects of the present.

Not only inspiration stands beside knowing your why. This type of question quickly spots causality to solve any problem. Questions of why lie down to manufacturing technique designed by the Japanese. It is better known as the 5 Whys method to find and solve problems. In other words, Toyota's scientific approach to manufacturing. Less idealism, more technicalities. The intelligent faculty gets on the massive scale. In making complicated things happen being positive and optimistic does not solve anything. The motive to move forward is not enough. Ineptitude is the barrier preventing from it. So focus on the details and causality is the way to solve problems. It recognises the cause and effect to fix a problem. After all, if something does not work - it has a reason. Moreover, if something does not work - it is a problem. Therefore, focus on the problem is the focus on the reason.

Problems slow down everything - solutions are accelerating. Technically, 5 Whys are the way to approach the core of everything. The centre where any inconvenience stems from. Especially valuable in solving problems. Instead of being caught by issues, questioning targets them to fix before they cause irreversible damage. The Japanese scientific way gives a practical design when the problem appears; the mind focuses on the reason which caused the problem. Then it removes the problem, turns down the issue and advances.

Such is the basic form given by questions of why. 5 Whys is the mode integrated in a questioning design already. No matter you repeat the question once, twice, five or twenty-five times. The pattern of questioning and its consistent application are what matters. Questioning is the skill, so the use of it will find a problem and will fix it. The longer you continue questioning, the higher the chance to dig deep enough to spot the reason. Looking at Toyota's success story, it is the way of approaching problems what contributed to it. For a practical application take a glide through this example:

1) Sales in the last quarter declined. Why?

2) Customers have shown less interest in the product. Why?

3) The product had some changes. Why?

4) Materials were changed. Why?

5) The single supplier did not deliver them as usual, so adjustments were made. Why…?

Therefore, in this case, sales in the last quarter declined because a single supplier did not deliver the usual order. This is a thought experiment where the questioning example is close to practice. In this case, the surface questions extract the problem from more profound levels. "Why" does not stop just with the number five to make the situation more transparent. Questioning focuses on what is not working, so it becomes clear what needs to be fixed. They apply as long as problems are solved, decisions taken and progress made. Better than Starting With Why is to begin with a question every time.

Moreover, repetitive whys act like the law of acuity. It penetrates deeper into the core of any problem. The deeper you go, the more layers of mystery you penetrate. Unseen levels become visible. Also, the further you go, the more difficult is to find answers to questions of why. The first answer to the question of why may be automatic. The second one becomes smart. The third looks thoughtful. The fourth - profound. The fifth approaches the core and so on. Unless it is a technical problem, the chain of processes is more straightforward than deep.

Eventually, triadic style there is the engine of making questions. The problem gives the context, and logic brings the structure and knowledge to fit the gap. Questions are compelling. With them, anyone has expansively no ends in development. There is always the chance to triple the perspective if you go in triadic style meticulously. The fitness of the verbal aspect promises an infinite expansion. Triadic style is to enlarge your view looking at least from three perspectives to any situation.

What is important that language is not only one expression of the mental architecture. Such government manifests itself in many other forms. Questioning at some point is wondering about things that you care about. Language is one of the modes to express your mind. There are works of art and music, writings, speeches, architecture, photography, gastronomy and many more. They have their forms to manifest themselves. As there are many countries, there are many constitutions of the mind. People are artists, writers, scientists, speakers, architects, photographers, food designers and so on. You do not see the mental architecture directly, but you can be sure when it gets expressed.

So questions are those to be expressed. Triadic style then is the verbal dress to the mental architecture. However, living in a complex and diverse world, triadic style is the symbol of the new outlook where everything gets questioned to make things better, faster, simpler and more beautiful. Triadic style goes for the whole idea of refinement and progress. Questions push things forward. Certain levels of balance are retained despite the strong acting. Daring nature will challenge traditional conventions. A bold character will challenge entrenched techniques. Fearless nature will challenge ordinary ways of doing things to make them extraordinary. Progress is the risky endeavour in the end.

Finally, the logic in quest touches many things. There are many openings for progress and refinement. What can you question to initiate progress? Everything - for example, agricultural traditions, manufacturing techniques, business processes, work ethics, art movements, dance forms, fashion trends, social models, economic doctrines, political ideologies, religious dogmas, scientific theories, etc. The most important is your immediate life. It receives questions to improve daily doings in the professional setting, social relationships, and personal level. In all environments, you have the mode to go with the logic in quest to make things different, better, simpler and more beautiful. The question-answer bridge shall bring confidence.

To question or not to question - that is the question. The question is the answer.

Askability Score
The Fitness and Utility

> *"Half of science is putting forth the right questions."*
> **Francis Bacon**

Questions are asked, answers are found - what is wrong on such fantastic ground? You already reached the point that questions lead the mind to think. Many would admit that overthinking is not the most actionable thing for their reasons. You remember that to question is to think. Then to over question means to overthink. Questions bring materials for thoughts - the more questions, the more ideas. It may seem evident that going in triadic style someone may pose questions unlimitedly. If someone applies triadic style meticulously, so one gets the ratio of 3:1. Every statement gets tripled because of what-how-why. It may lead to overthinking what many people do not like, but still get entangled. The Internet is full of articles on it what is partly the evidence of the struggle. Overthinking is not cool. So over questioning is not cool either. Questions shall intend for answers. Questioning just because you can is a part of another story. This is the crisis of triadic style which should not surprise us.

Overthinking is the starting road to confusion. You know where questology aims at - decisions and problems. The leadership of the question initiates thinking for it. The questioning pattern triples the number of potential answers. Questions go wild and force the mind into geometric expansion where it deviates from the target rather quickly. So it would distract from the objective and end up in confusion. Questions are answers; answers are squeezed and tripled until they outgrow into entanglement.

Over questioning may translate into overthinking. Overthinking is not the aim.

For the first reason, overthinking never gets cool because it does not solve problems. It thinks about problems heavily until it reaches the cognitive entanglement - the state where the mind gets stuck despite the activity. To find an analogy, it displays when someone gets in the quicksand without a hopeful chance. Overthinking seems very similar to thinking. The difference is that the act thinking goes forward, overthinking spins around. Repeating the same thought obsessively does not solve problems. Overthinking in such way is not helpful, so neither is the excessive questioning.

For the second reason, overthinking never gets cool because it does not make decisions. Many will demonstrate profound competence in hesitation. Indecisiveness is like someone who has plenty of options, but never picks one. Overthinking often leads to overthinking, and more overthinking points to itself. Not the direction forward, but a vicious circle. Considering that everybody needs or wants something - indecisiveness is the most remarkable way not to reach them. The mental architecture will interrupt, but there is another standard for governing questions.

For the third reason, overthinking never gets cool because it does not inspire change and progress. Repetitive thoughts of a single idea or the bunch of them rarely inspire for the action. It stimulates thinking instead. Overthinking means underacting. Where no action takes place, there is no consequence to close the case. Overthinking repeats itself and gives little value by building barriers to move forward. That is the moment what makes such thoughtful act uncool. Thinking must become visible or audible. Otherwise, it does not have much of practical utility.

The cognitive entanglement is the state of the mental confusion which shall be prevented. The easiest way to keep calm is to conduct thinking or establish the standard for questions. In other words, the discipline to make questions relevant and exclude the irrelevant. The management of questions will manage the mind. Questions are leaders of the mind, so if you start leading this leader, you will replace overthinking with productive thoughts.

To refine the issue, we introduce askability score to imply the value for questions. The standard to make them relevant or irrelevant. The relevant gets noticed and accepted while the irrelevant receive a silent treatment. Not every question is askable because time is limited. The most essential questions shall receive most of the time. The world is complicated enough to pay attention to everything that is neither productive nor rewarding.

Going forward, the excellent analogy of overthinking would be Twitter again. The abundance of tweets is to represent the intensity of questions having fun in overthinking's party. Twitter is not confusing though because it happens in front of you, not in you.

There are so many tweets going on every minute and second. For someone following thousands of people would be hard to listen. Complexity is the noise. The real confusion comes when there is no discipline to govern things. On Twitter, you can mute, or unfollow to filter the flow. Also, you can shut it down. In mind, for governing your thoughts is to establish the discipline.

This is a good analogy. Tweets represent thoughts - chaotically multiple. To manage them, you realign and govern settings. For another example, listening to 100 people talking in a different pace and volume will make the whole sound a little bit noisy and complicated. So then asking hundred of unrelated questions may bring similar trouble. Askability score is to rank questions even before they get asked - the standard to govern them. Problems or decisions - they are handled with the logic in quest. The standard to guide your attention and thoughts.

Then overthinking is complexity to be managed once the mind is managed. Overthinking is the noise you will remove by managing the mind. In this case, you receive fewer distractions. Irrelevant questions disturb, so askability score prevents from it by ranking questions. Then it brings a certain sense of awareness of what may be relevant for you already. This filters them and reduces the noise in mind. Instead of bringing noise, it fortifies your attention. This standard aligns questions towards a tailored direction as long as you keep asking them.

Some people are picky and preferential. It shapes their askability scores. Every question has a particular value for you as an individual. People who flirt with technology will put the higher score to questions about that. Equally, people who love food will prioritise these questions and thoughts. Sports, cars or stars - the same story. Directly, misaligning questions will get little regard. It sounds intuitive. Consequently, people will pay little attention to irrelevant questions. Likes and favourites are partial judges. The law of refinement is what removes unnecessary questions while askability score ranks them.

At this moment, there are few influencers making scores higher or lower. Fitness and utility of questions may be defined in specific metrics. First of all, curiosity and interest dictate and bring the decisive power to decide over which questions are relevant and which are not. Secondly, the context matters to influence askability score of individual questions. And, thirdly, those questions causing the highest impact receive the most significant value. Those influencers increase or decrease askability score for questions.

Influencers briefly:

Interest

Context

Impact

Three components deal with questions to play their role. They go for fitness and utility, so first and foremost, interest and curiosity shape your questions. This is a personal level. Preferences, backgrounds, and sympathies are the most obvious influencers to consider. Knowing yourself is the great asset to master this metric. Because it designs the standard. Nobody will tell you where your interests are or what are you curious about, but you. Interests are the starting point to acquire the standard which ranks questions. Exclude the best from the rest. And execute for answers.

When it comes to questions, naturally, people ask those which outshine others due to interest. Preferences and inclinations dictate askability score which is the assumed value of the question. So relevant and vital questions hold the highest value - you ask them first. And the opposite - of things you do not care about - you do not ask and even do not think about them at all. It starts making clear that preferences are a certain standard. In this context, fitness of the question is about ranking questions to target results.

Interest and curiosity are probably one of the reasons why things get done. It is natural to want something to be improving if you care about it. That is where attention goes and where you ask questions to get answers. Questions belonging to this sphere receives the highest priority. To accomplish anything remarkable means gathering rare and valuable answers. It becomes significantly harder to get there if someone lacks interest. Then such interest does not form questions, and without involvement, answers come harder regardless of ability to go in triadic style.

Having interests, what-how-why model gains a clear direction. Then, the function gets fit, or fitness gets functional. When both join together, you get fitting questions. With the purpose in mind, things are built, done or said for a specific goal. Bridges have their function, and buildings have it too. The function of the question is to get relevant answers. The function cannot tell you what fits. Merely mastering what-how-why does not mean it will find their fit soon. If it knew the direction, your mind would go there automatically, but initial intention and knowledge have to build interests first. Without it, problems and decisions are taken relatively harder compared where interests are clearly defined.

The fitness of the question establishes the standard. You are already aware of the natural role of your interests. Questions scale up their visibility. Relevance goes according to the standard. Worth noticing that there is no absolute standard. Something fits, but fitness does not apply to everyone. People have different interests, but what they have are interests - other ways to rank questions and move forward. Curiosity and interest are what matters there. Such thing ranks questions for the optimal outcome. You perhaps would not be satisfied wasting time on what does not matter to you. Finding out interests and follow up curiosity contribute to small progress - more relevant questions the better.

Interest and curiosity influence questions as well as answers. They affect the whole dynamics and fitness. When relevant questions get the priority, there is more likely for someone like you to accomplish what you care about. Mental energy is finite. The skill to pose questions will be useless if used purposelessly. It is curiosity and interest that draw a vector of mind forward. A perfect start for amplified focus because you naturally gravitate around things you are interested in. Hesitation to rank them up will cause ambivalence. It is not particularly useful.

That is about the personal department. Interests and curiosities are defined as private, so generally, fit on the individual level. Acknowledging this standard triadic style improves its focus. Meticulous questioning of what-how-why does not bring much of benefit if questions are irrelevant or unimportant to you. With this, you align your attention and priority. Knowing yourself is the asset for setting up this standard. If you do not know what interests or excites you, you probably need to ask questions and find it out. It influences askability score and prevents from overthinking after all.

Having no interest or being curious about nothing is just another way to pose questions. This invites a sweet paradox that even thought about lack of curiosity may make a person curious about the lack of curiosity. Where is it? The same applies to interest. The baseline to form a question is where intent and logic meets together to end up in a question. You need to have both. If one claims having zero interest is just a lack of awareness. The person perhaps is more interested in making others hear that one has no interests. Being interested in having no interests is waste of time. To solve the gap, one needs to observe what is done with the time. Then data comes uninvited, so the mind has the foundation to pose questions and move forward.

The next influencer is the context of the question. You perhaps do not find it surprising, but the place impacts the way you think. The modes of thinking influence the way you ask questions. The question is the bridge to the answer. So the direction of your lifetime partly depends on questions you ask and the place you are in. The context influences askability score, so some questions get verbalised and pursued while others are tagged as unfitting. The fitness of questions is quite straightforward - some of them do not fit in the context. Knowing this will be an advantage of pursuing what is relevant in where you are.

Friends, family, and fools are the excellent starting point to witness where the context come from. It forms an environment and ecosystem for thinking and acting. A person in the group of active people will get active as well. Or, if a person is being put in the enterprise environment, the mind will gravitate around relevant subjects accordingly. It is abundantly clear that things you do and say heavily depend on the context. The context is the influencing force shaping questions to be asked. The environment of close friends or strangers - in each of them different questions will get the priority. This makes the concept of askability score clear.

The priority is the authority for many things, not only askability score. Needless to say that the context influences what will potentially be done, said or thought of. The environment has a substantial impact on the mind. So the culture which circulates in the air fuels the attitude. Environments, the standard for questions are taken from there. Being in certain conditions reinforces a tacit social pact. For example, questions on free speech, capitalism or Human Rights in North Korea or Arabic countries do not align very much with the context there. In EU and the US, those questions would receive a better ranking in askability score because that is the part of the culture.

It must be evident that places influence the way you think. The most convincing reason why some people do not pose questions for their betterment is they were taught this way. Context sets up the standard. Some environments make some things unquestionable. If context makes nearly everything unquestionable, questions remain silent where thinking shrinks as well. Things get conventional, ordinary and simple what is an obvious progress' cripple. Questioning the normal shall be a new standard. For the dynamic tradition to restore the ambition and improve the condition.

Context is everywhere. Since you acknowledge the scale, it sets up standards. That is the culture for the mental architecture. For the question to fit the structure - it corresponds with context. Asking questions which do not fit in context equates to rocking the boat. Environment determines the rules things shall be going on. To violate the setting means to challenge the status quo. Thinking different than the standard guides may raise up the tides.

Sometimes the mind rebels against where the context is guiding to:

How is it possible that Galileo Galilei conflicted with orthodox belief to say that Earth is rotating around the Sun, not vice versa? It was not very askable at first.

How is it possible that Antoine Lavoisier rejected ancient teachings and introduced the role of oxygen to challenge phlogiston theory? It was not very askable at first.

How is it possible that Charles Darwin disagreed with the church dogma and formulated the principle of biological evolution? It was not very askable at first.

The list goes on…

Sometimes questions defined by the context are more static than progressive. Some environments invent the context which only accepts comfortable questions. Everyone will realise that comfortable questions inspire comfortable answers. You can only assume how far intellectual comfort or relaxed ambitions will lead. Although comfort is a preferably desired state of living, it preserves more than progresses. Asking questions out of context disagrees with the status quo and challenges rules of the game.

When it comes to existing standards, you know that the context provides a certain framework and rules to follow. History will present people and groups of people who had a strong impact on the world events. Either in science, technology, artistic or intellectual development - standards got challenged, and the world changed because individuals came up with greater standards that improved the society they thrived in.

Standards of science, technology, and intellectual development would suffer if individuals only agreed with the existing context without offering a better alternative. The world changes because engaged individuals or groups of them assemble where they forge standards better than the world can provide. Things they do may challenge the context. Moreover, questions sometimes are not well received because suggested standards do not match with existing ones. Standards of the world are not motivated to change, but they do change if they get challenged. Companies or individuals change the world because they develop a better standard than the world they operate in.

The standard is the context. Somewhere it is just done better. It is just more advanced. Show a smartphone to a caveman, and one will get angry and insecure for you challenged his comfortable beliefs. That is a provoking statement about the context. The context may be limiting and blinding playground because a different world may be unseen beyond the horizon. So rejected instantly.

It leads to the final influencer of askability score where the impact is the biggest. A potential impact of the question plays its part in askability score. Questions have their impact because they inspire for specific answers. For example, the question of how to find the cure for cancer has a higher impact than questions how to make tiramisu. Tiramisu is great, lovable and delicious. Having the answer for the formula for curing cancer is more impactful than knowing how to make tiramisu. A simple comparison of two potential answers. That is why questions towards those ends get compared with one another regarding their impact. And the higher the impact of the answer makes the question to become more askable and doable.

The impact of the question deals with the futuristic imagination. More than your interest and context, impact deals with the future. The tricky way to deal with such things because those are projections of the future. For example, knowing answer how to cure cancer is more impactful than the recipe of tiramisu. It distributes the difficulty of answers. Where answers are the most impactful, often they are the most difficult. There, questions are always connected to the future. Your mind travels in the future to compare perceived changes between now and then what means the comparison of impacts which influence askability score.

You neither see interest, context nor impact with your eyes. The mind's eye uses its sight for it. Askable questions express fitness - either the question fits or not - that is the standard to untangle overthinking. If to question is to think, then to over the question is to overthink. Askability score is the standard to manage questions and solve this issue. Ranking questions manage complexity in mind.

You set up the standard for complexity. Managing questions manages your mind. Focusing on interests removes the abundance, the context encourages questions to be asked. Also, the impact of the answer motivates specific answers to get the priority. Thinking forward is less overthinking. So questioning towards such direction has a similar output. That is where ability meets utility. Triadic style and askability score establish the logic in quest.

Chapter 7:
The Fourth Principle of Questology:
Complexity Management

"All generalisations are dangerous, even this one."
Alexandre Dumas

"Look with all your eyes, look."
Jules Verne

"Think like a man of action, act like a man of thought."
Henri Bergson

"Simplicity is the ultimate sophistication."
Leonardo da Vinci

You have already discovered standards and patterns which are assisting in deciding and solving problems accordingly. For now, it is not enough. However, it is often clever to design standards and have the method of justice for decision making. Standards are not absolute, but helpful for making them daily when the world floods you with complexity. Equally, the patterns of problems are something insightful. Every problem has its patterns where finding a solution destroys it and sends the problem to the graveyard.

When it comes to complexity, standards and patterns are highly valuable. The final fourth principle is for complexity which is naturally around. The reason why it arises in questology is that complexity management retains or restores the will to face the music. Either you understand and lead complexity, or it leads you to confusion and loss. Things are intellectual there; every mind can lose focus, so the quest for complexity management shall prevent from it.

It is exceedingly powerful to acknowledge the multidimensional approach. The world has a diverse climate, culture, and cities what shapes people in one way or another. It instantly designs the potential for various ideas because experience - where they stem from - is different. Seeing more layers of reality allows digging deeper things for a better understanding.

Initially, complexity management as a term firstly appears in business. There, the management of complexity has very definite consequences. It may lead to a significant increase in revenue or cost reduction. Both are the contributors to growth. The mental architecture is the excellent organisation to deal with complexity. That gives the hint of how to approach incoming complexity. What is equally important is to recognise it because complexity may have a negative impact while being covered in itself.

Growing company, wealth or oneself is growing nonetheless. To manage complexity perhaps the first quest is for learning.

Would be hardly relevant to manage things while keeping up in ignorance. Ignorance is not the tiger to make the fire. Knowledge is vital. There is always power dynamics - the mind is guided by itself or governed by complexity. With the logic in quest, everybody can pierce complexity like with a sword to get answers. One thing shall be intuitively held. Before managing anything practical; it shall be a self-commanding mind first. Personal government is the constitution to implement its standards and patterns because a lost person is not guiding oneself well.

Business management and mind's management are two distinct types of control. What unites business and the mind is management, only elements, and departments to manage differ. Mental management is its orderly thinking where business has different metrics to pursue. Behind every successful business, you will see excellent management practice. Behind every exceptional individual, you will find superb self-command. Moreover, behind every flourishing relationship, you will find committed coordination. Behind every productive work, you will see effective discipline. All areas have their complexity which is to be put on the single fabric.

Behind everything of value, you will find the fabric of quality. Complexity management has many forms. It becomes better defined and acted upon when the mind sees clearly. Therefore, the mind tames complexity by understanding it first. The quest for complexity management starts in mind. Everything great that has ever happened in history was because there was the mind so excellent that it put complexity into the mental model to produce something greater. Complexity is perplexing unless you know how to see.

Briefly, the multidimensional view is intimately connected with holistic thinking which may be trending. It is like having a multifaceted fabric where everything connects with everything. When complexity strikes, a single opinion has its disadvantages to understand what is naturally complicated. A singular view understands the part of complexity exactly to match the territory of the comfort zone. The rest of complexity remains uncovered and therefore missed. That is why it is so crucial to ask a question to lead yourself beyond a comfortable understanding. That is where you find a multidimensional pattern to expand the zone of comfortable thought.

Then, to manage complexity, despite it sounds naturally intuitive, one needs to learn things to solve problems and untangle what is twisted. Learning gives a necessary intelligence to discover patterns to problems and adjust standards to make decisions. Initial knowledge is vital for understanding of problems before you can answer it. Equally, before any quality decision, facts and figures bring you information. Learning and questioning are the way to approach and reshape the comfortable.

While learning is natural and expansive - the opposite may have its little flaws. When you think of expansion, compare a person who learns things and someone who does not. Learning things expands your understanding and assists in problem solving. Such is an integral part of complexity management. The mind evolves by learning, so it can solve problems which hide their intricate patterns. Any refusal to learn brings to the situation when a person gets its tiny comfort zone threatened by complexity.

However, learning sometimes misguides the learner. It is evident that a person can learn things that do not work, is distorted or just fabricated. This is the part where learning is not as useful as it shall be. Everyone knows what indoctrination is. It twists perception to be superior to reality - it explains why so many people prefer to fly with prejudice than to touch the ground. Learning false is taxing what misguides the mind for struggles. The mind gets tricked.

Then there comes the moment to remove such cosmetics from the mind for it to face the music as it plays. Comfortable knowledge is comforting while painful truths are challenging. Over the choice between prejudice and reason, everyone can make a stand. Before the decision, one shall discover both sides of the matter through questions. When both sides are examined, a person can be sure one is better informed. To manage complexity, one needs to understand it to release oneself from the comfort zone or liberate the comfort zone from prejudice.

You will realise that learning may be useful, neutral as well as harmful. Learning misleading figures, theories and opinions can quickly bring you where you do not like to be. That is where, to manage complexity of the world, one needs to untangle complexity in the head at first. The step of detachment is the suspension of knowledge for the mind to tackle everything

Eventually, when the mind dissects oneself from learning, it is open for going light. Where learning has no luggage, and so the mind will operate swiftly. Complexity is entangling, so disentanglement from it shall be solving it. Comfortable existence does not challenge complexities around, but guards its territory. The fabric of understanding is the surface and universe to approach the reality that everything connects with everything. Having a tiny comfort zone is just a small universe on the complex fabric. Complexity is complex - not a cheerful walk in the spring.

The Complex Fabric of Understanding

"Principles for the development of a complete mind:

study the science of art. Study the art of science.

Develop your senses - especially learn how to see.

Realise that everything connects to everything else."

Leonardo da Vinci

Imagine, you are walking in the park, so you go forward to the road. The question is whether your feet hit the road or the road hits your feet by going on its own. Perhaps it is the road that goes under you? Two approaches quickly come to realise that there is more than one way to look at things. The relative path now seems to be common sense due to achievements Albert Einstein had made. It was not so common before him. So either you walk across the way, or this way moves under you - two approaches to open up the gates to multidimensional thinking.

Many of us know the story about an optimistic-pessimistic glass. When the glass is half filled, pessimists see it half empty while optimists claim it half full. Often people see what they want to see - comfort zone is issuing this way of seeing. As to analogy, the glass stands there with some water in it. Perceptions build lenses to see the world. No matter the glass, you will fulfil it despite its first giving. You could not care less in falling into a popular division between optimists and pessimists - they have their lenses of vision to perceive the world. Let them own it. Attitudes are the perspective - optimistic, pessimistic or whatistic - they affect the way of looking at the world. You could be whatistic - for the sake of difference whatever it means. All of them are questionable as all of them may be quite practical.

Clothing for your mind to wear could be sophisticated enough. What is unique about such thing is its invitation to see the world from a broader perspective. Precisely, treating reality as if it appeared through a kaleidoscope. It is neither right nor wrong, but insightful what is needed to see issues from various angles populated on multidimensional fabric. One thing to be clear. Regarding problem solving, it would be foolish to hold either right or wrong attitude. Much more valuable is to solve the problem rather than demonstrate righteousness. It is not whether someone is "right", but whether one solves the problem or not.

Regarding complex problem solving, Albert Einstein said, you cannot solve the problem on the very same level of thinking it appears. You will notice those occurring new problems are to challenge the intellect at the time they happen. If things were easy, problems would not be called problems. If any problem appears along the way, it brings inconvenience to be removed.

The complex fabric of understanding populates a diversity of standpoints to extract alternative solutions. The gates for insights to evolve faster than problems do to solve them. Multidimensional fabric adds to the mind fresh ideas and new opportunities. It does not remain in the territory of comfort then. Something valuable for complexity management because complexity begins where your comfort ends. When you understand the multifaceted aspects of reality, there is easier to see the interconnectedness among things.

There is a huge difference between a single dimension and multidimensional. Reading books is the very classic escape from the moment of now. Almost everyone can read stories of previous centuries or imagined futures. The work of fiction brings fuel for imagination to submerge oneself into the literary work. That being said, you will see the parallel dimensions going forward simultaneously. The one someone is reading the book and another where the plot of the book carries the mind. Two realities are going on the complex fabric.

Another excellent example is for current technologies taking the edge. Virtual reality is an entirely immersive experience of the world. The world which looks real, yet exists once simulated. It is not hard to see the distinction between two different dimensions. For the visual example, a person stands in the room wearing such immersive glasses where virtual reality happens in the physical one. This is not the question to answer in this book. What matters more than that is to sober up the mind to show that there is always more than one way to look up at things.

Even dreaming is a good example. Everybody sleeps nowadays. Who does not - either lies or dies. As one among many displays of other perspectives. Moreover, drinking changes the view, as well as entertainment does. Also, involvement in games or culture has a similar effect. There are many causes to influence the change of perspective and understanding. It has a positive impact which brings insights and encircles problems. Seeing them from many sides refreshes a dull repetition.

You will find it intuitive, but it is quite rare to solve things you do not understand. So the holistic approach is to widen up your understanding and push for solutions. For instance, looking at the facade of the building may reveal no problem if the problem happens to be internal. Unfortunate if it is the only way you see. The single-minded approach may see only one face of the situation. Keeping within the personal opinion is not the most courageous act. Even the most righteous standpoint is useless unless it solves problems. A deeper understanding shows more than one face of the problem.

We have many cultures with their traditions. Members of any finely selected society are taught to have a certain mindset. Either it is European, American or Asian - thoughts and actions are often guided by tradition which serves as a compass. The compass of traditional patterns governs someone's life. Being immersed in a single culture will bring specific values - glasses to see the world through. You see the diversity which is one part of the story. Conventional patterns are open for enrichment.

You should not confine yourself to one culture only. Other factors amplify the difference in thinking as well. You do not need to jump across distant cultures and continents, and there are more influences to impact your fabric of understanding. You may find economists, scientists or lawyers in a very dense area. Even in the same city. Their training brings them the unique mindset and knowledge.

This part is interesting. Being immersed in backgrounds experts represent knowledge sets they are in. Professional methods they apply and knowledge differ from one expert to another. All experts have a common logic behind specialisation. They shall be proud of their profound exposure to their fields. The interesting point is that specialised knowledge is only one among many others on the complex fabric of understanding. Being a specialist allows managing complexity within the field.

You know that fields connect with one another - they do not live alone. For complexity management, it is not enough to see things within the field. Expansive thinking guides out the common understanding put in the box. Complexity is well present between specialisations. Chemistry is chemical, biology is natural, engineering is practical while biochemical engineering becomes interesting. It displays complexity between fields.

So complexity is twofold. One stands in the field. A chemist is a profession, a biologist is too as well as an engineer. What puts understanding out of singular box there is the biochemical engineer. Just a name where forced connection to put three elements under one equation to get the complex one. This is only one random example. You will discover yourself a constant increase in complications - within the field and among them.

That is where the multidimensional fabric will serve as the analogy to put complexity on. Complexity happens in between various areas which are divided and fluid on the complex fabric. More than culture and special knowledge, the organisation of knowledge is way more interesting. For example, economists and scientists may have a very similar mental architecture where elements are the difference. That will be the link between two different fields. An economist would know economic history; a scientist will know history of science - various shades of the complex world.

What is the economic model for the economist, for the scientist would be a scientific theory. They look at the world, but see particular aspects of it - in the way they were trained to look at it. There are many parallels where principles of science are operated by the scientist and laws of economy guided by the economist. Professionalism is built on the common logic. Two universes which are closer than it seems - on the complex fabric.

You need to realise that people's mind is profoundly affected by the backgrounds. Cultural background is one field, knowledge is another. At the same time, there is a huge diversity both in cultures and expertise. They give glasses to look at the world to make it multidimensional. That is where you get the term of complex thinking in the first place. Moreover, to realise an economist's way of thinking, it is about understanding the pattern. To achieve scientists' way of thinking - the pattern is the case.

It helps to convert one way of thinking into another which transcends a personal opinion as the situation requires. For asking better questions to solve problems, you need to understand different aspects of reality. Problems do not care about you. If you cannot solve them, you cannot. Unless the question broadens up the perspective and hits the answer. Comfortable questions will hit comfortable answers which are never larger than common sense.

Everybody is capable of seeing a building when it is in front. The limitation of a single approach quickly invites a restriction. For example, being outside, the interior is out of sight. At the same time, being inside the building, the interior is obvious, but the exterior becomes out of vision. Many things could be treated this way because they have specific interior and exterior settings. Attitude shall be light enough to pierce the problem from the inside out and outside in.

In the complex environment, there is no right solution but only what fits. The fitness comes from workability. You know perfectly well that to reach the centre of any city thousand ways are to be found. The same applies to problems. The optimal path would be the straightest one, yet many lead towards the solution. That being said, there are no absolute solutions but those which fit. Fitness is determined not by righteousness but for suitability. For the finalising analogy - you cannot open up the chest because you think you own the right key. Only when the key fits, the chest opens. The same applies to problems and solutions.

What is the opposite of multidimensional thinking is the comfort zone - the territory of a single approach. Complexity outside is indeed staggering compared to the tiny comfort zone. Familiar knowledge and training without further learning do not expand much. As for someone sees the world, thinks and acts in the way one got familiar. The reason why comfort zone may be static is that it preserves more than progresses. It is safe and sound. To think and act differently is dangerous. A single opinion is comfortable. Comfort is hostile to change. Progress is uncomfortable because it changes the comfort.

For ability to convert one dimension to another and apply knowledge, learning is essential. Otherwise, there is nothing to translate and nothing to use. Complexity is out of sight remaining its threatening face. You will spot different patterns, once you understand patterns of things. The acquisition of the first patterns comes from learning. Profoundly devoted learning is the excellent starting point for seeing that everything connects to everything else.

Acquiring knowledge solves problems indirectly unless you learn the solution. You know that innovation and problem solving are intimately connected. Some problems get solved through innovation and innovations happen while solving problems. In situations when you are unable to solve a problem, the improvement of mind shall be the goal. New complex problems often are not solved on the same level because complexity of the mind sometimes does not match complexity of the new problem.

Then learning brings new ideas, fresh perspectives and complex derivations of the new from the old. When the mind gets upgraded, complexity becomes threatened. It shall not bother you. It means while your mind is being improved, problems remain in the comfort zone. Higher beats lower, so complexity gets a disadvantage and therefore gets managed.

The advantage comes from seeing the world from a multidimensional perspective where everything connects with everything else. Some groups brainstorm, question assumptions or exercise forced connections to gather ideas and change the fabric of things. Then ideas, methods or products are open for reinvention and reconnection. Different perspectives meet on the same ground. That is a multidimensional fabric where the diversity strikes in. Such things boost current opportunities to surround problems till their surrender.

Talking on innovation and novelty, to make the salad you combine fruits. Brainstorming sessions are the excellent way to gather individuals to enrich perspectives hoping that something newer will follow. A solution, insight or the element. Many metrics to be found. Regardless of the intention, brainstorm has its benefits and disadvantages. The benefits amplify the number alternatives on the table. The downside may come when there are many alternatives to cause a slight complexity.

Brainstorming creates opportunities and initiates solutions. Beside brainstorm, someone is open to connect elements forcedly. An elementary example will involve obvious mathematics behind. For example, you will take numbers to make 1+1=2. Two numbers were connected against their will. They could not protest, so they did not mind. This example implies action. Despite its rudimentary state, it is the beginning point to amplify the potential to get something more useful. The problem with such mathematics - it is analytical while life is real.

Mathematics is not the best method to engage in creative endeavours. It brings a strong foundation against complexity and stands for precision. Despite being the agent of precision, mathematics will translate its inner working into other dimensions without asking any permission. Everyone can connect 1 and 1 to make 2. It is weird this is even talked about. Take the same actions and what can happen if you join a computer with a telephone? Or let's say metal and bird into something singular? You may get a smartphone or an airplane for this demonstration.

In the forced connections, numbers get replaced by more familiar practical objects to stimulate innovation. All sets of ideas and things are possible to be bridged to extract something remarkable. Connecting at least two distinct ideas the third forms eventually. Before you combine them, you might have been exposed to learning and those backgrounds. Take more examples under the equation. Elements are forcedly connected when:

To get a mermaid (from Disney movies), you join parts of a woman with pieces of a fish.

To get a centaur (like Firenze from Harry Potter), you join parts of a human with elements of a horse.

To get a pegasus (from Disney movies), you join parts of a horse with parts of the bird.

And so on…

Two distinct elements are joined to extract something different and perhaps creative. What looks like magic have invisible structures behind. Seeing no structures and aware of no patterns everything may look like magic. What seems unreal and imaginary there may get real. In case of forced connections - those creatures are magical and in the movies. However, advanced genetic engineering could make them. Advanced science becomes magic. The question will be if such manipulations are needed.

Not magical creatures are what you need, but the elementary approach. It is not a superpower - it is a fabric of mind where things are treated like elements and acted upon accordingly. New connections in mind build new bridges for you to get out of familiar island.

You are already approaching to realise that a familiar island is only one dimension to look at things. If there is nothing, but one little island which happens to be the point of view, then there is nowhere to depart. The multidimensional fabric is the playground for many dimensions. Then, the edge of the comfort zone is not the end of the world. Beyond the horizon, there are more layers and perspectives to discover. Getting out of personal bubble is the metaphorical way to explore the unknown. Questions lead the mind as a compass does.

The reason we mentioned some inventive ways to create novelty is to escape from boundaries of a single opinion. Then brainstorming, forced connection or questioning sound like expansive acts to get away the limitation of personal opinion. The intricate part that to even start connecting something with something, there is one requirement. It must be the first intelligence to connect with. That is the place, where learning comes at hand. No matter in which form, it provides knowledge and information to serve as building blocks and clay.

Multidimensional thinking expands the vision in exchange for the price. The broader the perspective, the less focus. Modes of thinking change on a pulsating command where the mind guides itself. You may know those people operating on different mental designs - fastidious on details, and inspiring in ideas. Multidimensional thinking is broad; the focus is sharp. The radical switch to one or another is the death of the synergy. Then, either person gets imprisoned in a personal cave or is unable to sustain attention. Like interior and exterior complexities in the world.

Finally, the derivation of new knowledge and applying them in practice makes it more comfortable. Comfort extends when complexity shrinks. The size of complexity is directly dependent on the comfort zone. So the size of the comfort zone defines the levels of complexity. There is a constant battle between those two. Multidimensional thinking may stop a blind flirtation with an entrenching idea, so the mind will move forward. Opinion is common, logic is rare. Both logic and opinion come from learning. Ignorance does not solve problems. Ignorance is not the tiger to make the fire. For complexity management, you have to learn before you make the tables turn.

Learning as Electricity of Progress

> *"An investment in knowledge pays the best interest."*
> **Benjamin Franklin**

The multidimensional approach puts extra layers of understanding like the outfit. The structure of logic and fitness of questions craft the logic in quest. The mobile act of penetrating things flexibly and navigating the mind despite complexity. Now as you remember the dressing up of the mind, logic stands for the structural component. The verbal approach brings mobility to your mind, and so questions get mobilised to move your mind forward.

You must realise that learning is electricity of progress. Just imagine someone who was a complete ignorant. Knowing nothing brings little chance to combine knowledge to squeeze the juice of something remarkable. Then complexity is like a tornado to give you a high five and suck you in. Without knowledge, there is nothing to connect and not much to think about. Then complexity becomes the master to cause you a beautiful disaster. Learning electrifies and refreshes the mind to do things it did not do before. Like the fuel for the engine to work. Many will praise education as the rescue from ignorance and the stand against complexity.

Like the old saying goes when money makes money, so knowledge makes knowledge. We embrace another approach which does not contradict, but put the focus on different priorities. The known thing says that it is hard to make money without initial investments. Compound interest is a well-known amplifier of affluence. Is not knowledge another asset of wealth? Itself it inevitably generates nothing. Once applied it creates consequences. Knowing how to do things while others do not is the way to play the game. Then it becomes enjoyable, profitable and rewarding. Knowing is similar to owning capital. The value shows up in use.

Knowledge and intelligence are capital. Moreover, having no understanding of how capital works leads to its loss. Obvious why intelligence is praised because it knows how to behave with complicated things. Intelligence manages complexity. The starting point to get there is to learn new things which enable the mind to grow and get applied. Learning and research are the gateway to knowledge, wealth building and making complexity insecure.

Speaking metaphorically, learning is like cultivating your garden. Your knowledge is to represent such metaphor. There are plenty of things to see, hear, smell, taste or touch. Anything from direct experience to the most abstract speculation. Putting knowledge in your head is like growing plants. For the visual representation, the garden metaphor fits very well. Individual then resembles a garden populated with diverse ideas and fulfilled with experiences. The more resourceful your personality, the more populated the garden. Where is the gardener?

Learning is always directional. When someone learns anything, he or she has a purpose in front. For example, someone goes to university to get a degree to find employment. The purpose makes learning directional. Learning without a clear goal sounds like entertainment. But even self-entertainment is directional. Otherwise, time and mental energy would be spent elsewhere. The absence of direction quickly invites complexity for dinner. That is where the logic in quest shall manage the course of your mind. Focus beats the noise of information where the leadership of the question takes a stand.

There is always something to learn or derive learning, discover and invent. What is more important than education is a derivation of new knowledge. Like growing new plants in the metaphoric garden. Elements of knowledge are not equal. For example, knowing how to turn on a computer and knowing how to extend the human lifespan differ a bit. Enrichment comes in many forms. When you treat your mind like a garden, knowledge represents plants.

The dangerous part comes for gardens get infected or weed growing. The mind will follow the same path. Everyone shall act as an experienced gardener to prevent such things from happening. Your mind may get polluted or infected. This is the garden after all, so everyone shall care about what one is growing. As you follow this metaphor, knowledge is like plants in the garden. Let's assume the mind is busy in cultivating them. To derive new knowledge and enrich understanding would sound like being a better gardener. New knowledge - new plants. Learning, experimenting and educating oneself is the great beginning for it. Such an act is a good example to begin deriving new knowledge.

Learning the ropes is the necessary thing to put something on the top after. To extend knowledge starts with the question. The question builds upon what you know and targets what you do not know. The derivation when old and familiar outgrows into new and unfamiliar. Future contains answers; questions are made now. They are the initiative to connect with answers hanging out in the future.

Future is where all possible derivations of knowledge take place. What is left to do is to pose questions to advance. At the same time, you cannot ignore actions. It is clear that growing plants in the garden requires effort, so the whole thing of acquiring knowledge demands energy as well. Energy is as infinite as that one in the battery. Learning everything depletes it. Questions are good initiators to execute your priorities.

Focus and question then. For a slight reminder, questions delegate the mind to go for what is important and relevant. This derives your attention and put on your energy. All this is intuitive. But even intuitive things get covered with complexity, so become invisible until they are pointed out again. Learning is the primary source to taste the reality. Without the first knowledge, it becomes a substantial disadvantage for there is nothing to advance. So derivation and use of knowledge then become taxed and burdened.

In deriving new knowledge, the territory of comfort expands leaving less space for complexity to cause a disorder. Complexity contains problems. The problem-free world does not exist unless it is perfect. Give something perfect to someone, and one will want more. Wanting more is not the problem. The problem is in between you and your ambition. To solve the problem means to jump over the barrier separating you from the aim.

In this context, learning gravitates around solving. A solution is what you may be missing. Learning the solution is one of the ways to reach it out. It seems natural that learning the solution and applying it immediately solves the problem - a convenient end of the learning process. For entering any new arena, to learn solutions shows previous problems and memorable ways how they were solved. Knowing how to manipulate knowledge solves things.

Learning solutions to problems is easy. To learn and to know is no longer enough. There is no benefit in being a billionaire if wealth is in no use. As well as being a walking library does not bring enough value if knowledge remains unused. Knowledge is useful if applied and useless if not - what is the use then? Familiar solutions then match familiar problems like the glove matches the hand.

Generally, to learn an answer is easy. Everybody does it. The issue starts when problems arise to which there is no solution to learn. Something new is challenging. Things in the memory cannot match the problem in the way the glove matches the hand then. So another approach is open for a go.

To learn to solve is another step of advancement. Learning is for solving. Something applicable. In situations where solutions are not available to learn, the problem becomes bigger than the size of the comfort zone. In this way, learning is about solving. When there is no solution to the problem, then learning the problem gathers the intelligence to design the solution. That is why learning the problem is a thing. The focus accelerates understanding. It is rare to solve something intricate without understanding the complexities of it.

Emerging technologies are a good example to represent arising problems in the industries never existed long time ago. Knowing how to solve problems is more than knowing solutions to them. That is the difference. Many advancements in technology will provide challenges to be addressed. A number of them will resemble situations where the glove does not match the hand, so solutions will be designed uniquely for problems.

What is more important than learning solutions is the pattern. For example, learning solutions to 100 unique problems is an excellent sign of expertise. More than that, knowing how to solve problems represents the pattern which will know how to behave with every problem. This is more than 100.

Learning enables to see the invisible - the pattern itself. To learn patterns, you need to master the art to deal with information and complexity. Then information spins around the pattern which acts as a functional algorithm. In the Information Age, to remain competitive, someone needs to learn the art of how to solve problems which were never solved before. Existing information will provide solutions for previous problems, yet complexity will increase in newly arising problems. Everyone can get information, but only some will tackle issues where information has not been recorded. Then you learn to solve. Intelligence is applied, not owned.

Knowledge is the source of power to put pressure on the future. To learn a solution or to learn to solve are sides of the same coin. One needs to take advantage of both. Initial knowledge is capital to design a question for the further one. From there, questions will target what is unknown yet. You have met the leadership of the question already. Having some intelligence, questions lead your mind to think and aim at what is hidden. Knowledge expands when questioned. Seeing the horizon is common, but questions lead out of comfortable understanding. Then you learn new things.

The plot twist comes when learning and knowledge start building the future. Like in any construction works, materials are the part of the process. To create the future which does not exist, you will need knowledge you do not have. Knowledge is the building material. Then you need to learn to start putting pressure on the future. Learning builds the foundation for questions which are the force to lead held understanding forward. To get knowledge you do not have - you ask questions you never did.

Moving forward, for solving problems, making decisions or developing anything, learning and research serve as the foundation. It extends logic you use and opinions you hold. People think like lawyers, chemists or architects most likely because they got exposed to such subjects as law, chemistry or architecture. Such are their gardens. Moreover, thinking like the scientist, economist or the artist - are interesting outcomes. Mindsets are designed to govern information - each specialist does it. This serves as professional guidance through complexity. That is why experts think in the way they do. This is where you witness unique designs of the mental architecture.

Exposing to new arenas brings the input into the complex fabric of understanding to see things from many angles. The multidimensional approach will tell you that the same information will get treated differently by the scientist, economist or an artist. You see this interconnectedness when specialists behave in their fields. Mental design interprets the world according to its standard. So depending on the background, the world appears in a specific colour. Knowledge and information become elements to be governed by mental patterns owned by experts.

Take a deeper glide. When knowledge of economy connects with a person, one becomes a trained economist. Moreover, when understanding of science connects with the person - one is a trained scientist. And there are many ways to acquire a professional attitude. When someone gets educated, one receives a specialised set of knowledge which forms thinking patterns. Patterns are invisible - that is why one needs to learn how to see.

Special learning assists in dealing with complexity. Knowledge sets are built to deal with the world. Thinking like an economist or having scientific thinking patterns bring distinct views for individuals. You see the main idea. Learning develops a certain mindset which defines the way to manipulate information.

Think of this. You extract a particular equation to define the potential for multidimensional fabric. When a human connects with a specialised set of knowledge - it bakes a professional. Special knowledge is profound, but limited. General knowledge lies widely around, but lacks depth. Connecting scientific knowledge with a person, human remains - scientist prevails. In this way, the person adopts a mental design of the scientist. If this is possible, then other modes of thinking shall be available as well.

Watch this:

Human + Science = Scientist

Human + Economy = Economist

Human + Law = Lawyer

Human + Architecture = Architect

Human + Medicine = Medic

Etc.

An obvious connection of a person with a specific set of knowledge - it bakes a professional. There is no limit reached - there are multiple dimensions of knowledge. Learning basics are the first step to understand other backgrounds as well. As someone is capable of acquiring sets of knowledge, one is completely capable of jumping from one set to another. People do expand their point of view by learning. When a human learns science, one grasps the scientific way of thinking. While someone acquires knowledge of law, one understand the way how lawyers think. But what can happen if someone combines many areas of knowledge? For example:

Human + Science + Economy + Law + Architecture + Medicine + etc. = ?

Sounds like integrating the complex fabric of understanding into a person. Then it becomes more of jumping across different fields by learning. Leaving one set and entering another. There is a thing to recognise. Various sets of knowledge allow an initial grasp of them. The way multidimensional fabric gets its way there is because it encircles the problem from many angles. Looking at the professional challenge, for example, there are many ways to approach it. Lawful, economic and scientific understanding offer other patterns what expand single-minded approach. The higher chance to squeeze the solution of the complex problem is when a broader vision is taken place.

Again, developing ideas is like cultivating a garden. For a visual example, garden fits perfectly well to represent ideas similar to the cultivation of plants. A devoted gardener knows that leaving a garden poorly cultivated will inspire the growth of unpleasant weeds. The abandoned mind generates similar thoughts. In this context, the different set of knowledge represents distinct gardens. Metaphorically, the content in mind is different from one professional to another. Like the two gardens are different. Everyone can learn foreign things like some plants were wild initially.

The mind is to receive excellent gardening practice. Good practice prevents from weed pollution. And the cultivated garden is more admirable than an abandoned one. Not only for aesthetics, but also for functionality. So this is the different line where the new knowledge will get derived. Learning and joining knowledge of various backgrounds open up the potential for novelty veiled from your eyes. Then, someone like you gets open to understanding other patterns of other fields. It is advantageous in solving problems. Various sets of knowledge join into a single unity to surround the struggle and squeeze it to surrender.

You know that any finely selected set of knowledge is functional. Suited for a specific purpose. Knowledge of science serves for understanding and making use of the physical world, law for serving justice, architecture for building constructions and so on. People specialise and then fulfil their specialisations. Such knowledge is special.

Research in different arenas expands the aptitude needed for solving complex issues. It is intuitive that special knowledge is for special problems. Complex knowledge applies to complex problems. The world is complex by the way. Learning extracts practical ability, but thinking patterns are more expensive. To solve a problem, one shall be more of an excellent problem solver than a knowledgeable person. Thinking patterns are vital; knowledge is special - that is the relationship between principal and practical.

Both learning and thinking take mental energy. For the mastery of known things, they cost effort and time. Like growing plants in the garden, learning often requires patience. What you need is to take knowledge with you. The serious part starts when you master enough knowledge to convert it from one dimension to another. Take elements of it and combine with other elements from other sets. As you have seen in multiple examples to derive new learning, it requires some forced connections by taking part from one knowledge set and combine with another set. The phone and the computer perfectly connect in a single smartphone you make use of. It starts when elements from different backgrounds meet up forcedly or willingly.

Moving forward, answers are what you need. Questions are where you start. Your will is how you exercise. Questions are the supreme force in making small derivations from current knowledge. Learning is vital in the beginning because it fuels and converts into thinking and acting. Having a grip on history, the arts and sciences, medicine, mathematics, philosophy, economics, music, law, technology, etc. is expansive. It does not stop there. For thinking from various angles, such input dramatically improves seeing things from multiple perspectives. The disadvantage comes when someone sees only one side of the coin. Someone fails to follow curiosities, refuse to learn and prefers to stay in the cave like a brilliant caveman. One rubs sticks to make a fire while others design rockets to explore space.

To derive new knowledge and enrich any field requires more than just being able to learn and understand. Isaac Newton once said that if he had any seen any further, it was by standing on the shoulders of giants. Learning and heritage are addressed. Newton is considered to be one the most influential scientist of all times. An outstanding intellectual and scientific figure to mention. It represents the mode of thinking about the principles. To learn what is known and derive what is not known sounds like a modern research project. Something unknown becomes known. What one man discovers another can learn. And to discover one needs to learn in the first place. That is good for questioning after.

Then, Newton becomes an example of the mental effort and insight. He is a pensive figure of admiration. One of his discovery may seem romantic. Notably, the one of the falling apple one of which Voltaire - French writer - brought to Europe and helped to popularise. You can only guess how this connects with current MacBooks, iPads, and iPhones. Just an act of the apple falling down the tree - an insight which brought understanding of gravity in the easy and elegant form. For the exceptional mind ordinary acts becomes the extraordinary ending.

Multidimensional thinking will find hidden connections between insights. Exposure to deep and broad learning is the starting point for rare connections. In this case, you can only guess how this romantic explanation may look like. Apples look like planets - similarity comes in form. Plain laws of association jump from one dimension to another. Seeing an apple falling, the question then is how about planets and solid bodies in general? They may act similarly because they share similar properties. To associate, one needs to be in two modes of thinking. Then the plain act of apple falling may be the ground for universal gravity. The discovery unknown before. What one man discovers, another can learn it.

More practical example of deriving novelty is Thomas Edison. Many will know that he is considered to be a well-known inventor and businessman. Practicalities receive stronger emphasis than the theoretical approach in this case. Practical inventions are more realistic than gravity despite many obey it in practice. Newton remains pensive while Edison is the man of active and inventive energy. It is the achievement made out of trial and error to end up with a commercially viable light bulb. Discoveries and inventions enlighten the world. If you do not believe it - turn on the light in your room at night to make it bright.

Thomas Edison is relevant for his energy where he brought ideas into practice. He was more practical than pensive. He developed many valuable devices for the world including the phonograph, the motion picture camera, and a commercially viable light bulb. Holding 1093 inventions under his name, Edison represents the man of invention. That is where he differs from Newton. Edison guided less energy on what is fundamental and had done what is practical. That is perhaps one among the reasons why Edison is known more of an inventor than a discoverer of new concepts. What one man invents another can use.

For gravity, it existed even before Newton formulated it in a comprehensive form. After this, it becomes a part of the education programs where people learn what once was discovered. Similar to Edison, what one man invented, others can learn. Learning is more comfortable than thinking, but both make their contributions. To think one needs to learn otherwise there is nothing to think about. Similarly applies to inventions - before reinventing something one needs to learn and test. Otherwise, it would resemble the state of being in the process of inventing something that is already created. Things are to be reinvented or thought of differently. If it was easy, everyone would do that.

Learning goes first, thinking pattern comes second. Then thinking patterns start leading knowledge. Thinking is superior to learning, but learning is vital for thinking. If someone did not learn anything, what he or she shall think about? Discoveries and inventions enrich and contribute to the society. Learning things, applying knowledge and getting results is what makes society progressive. Learning and the constant application is the matter to keep the mind active. What you will discover, others will learn. Knowledge may be leading to discovery. At the same time, things you may create or invent others can use. Sounds like advancement unless you prefer to repel yourself from curiosities. More important than learning is doing, but learning is electricity to use - everything else is the novelty to deduce.

Mental Property Taxes
&
The Cognitive Entanglement

> *"There is no such thing*
> *as a good tax."*
> **Winston Churchill**

As you know, learning is like cultivating your garden. The main problem is the threat of weeds rather than flowers. In the natural gardening practices to grow something remarkable requires care, work, and attention. Otherwise, there is the grave risk to pollute oneself. That is where learning may be progressive, admirable as well as harmful. Learning brings things to your mind. Pulling things ravenously without care and attention give more property than needed. There is the potential place for complexity to introduce itself. So the mind collects knowledge for no use. Knowledge is useful, worthless or poisonous. The effect on the present and the future is evident.

First of all, it could not be more evident that specific knowledge is just vital for practicalities. Essential knowledge and skill for the job are immediately applied. Learning for earning - useful knowledge brings value in practice. Not necessarily work-related learning gets its attention. Employing skills into practice achieves practical results. Let's be explicit - useful knowledge brings value.

Secondly, you must realise that not everything you learn is equally useful immediately. Keeping value as the standard, you will say that what does not bring value is worthless. Learning Latin is not particularly practical despite its reputation and benefits for the mind. Latin has once been a part of classical education, for now, is not considered a precious type of knowledge. Learning any other practical set of knowledge would be more useful. It requires time and dedication. However, the experience which is joyful for itself is valuable - only the standard is different then. Such standard is not practical in the end what makes knowledge somewhat neutral.

Thirdly, the most important, there is a type of knowledge which receives serious attention. Poisonous knowledge is neither valuable nor remains neutral. Acquiring this kind would be particularly toxic for the mind's health. This is the source where prejudice, false theories, and alternative facts stem from. For a definition, poisonous knowledge is deluding the mind when it accepts things for real even though they have something to conceal. Alternative facts and fake news are among examples. This type of knowledge will quickly tax the mind and cause the conflict with reality. The mind gets confused because it learns what is misleading.

When you consider the complex fabric of understanding, one potentially will translate patterns of one department to another. Learning foreign ideas make them native. For example, the translation of physics to psychology. Precision is debatable though. However, following this logic, what works in physics shall work in psychology as well. Just take some popular ideas from the best selling books. The law of attraction finds its foundations in gravity coined by Newton. Theories of personal development find its support in the theory of evolution. Positive thinking finds its replacement in electromagnetism where electric charge makes something positive or not. Fundamentals of physics convert into psychology. Is it convincing?

This is debatable. Physics and psychology are disciplines of different fields. Physics deals with reality while psychology is busy with the perception of it. Regarding reality, physics is primary while psychology remains second after physics. Psychological conclusions may be more important and comforting people. Then, psychology is more social than physics while physics is more natural. Everyone can construct the social universe because it is inventible. Relationships between people are equally complex like laws of physics. Admittedly, the social realm is dynamic and less stable. To break up the relationship and social laws is easier than breaking up gravity between the Earth and the Moon for instance.

Look what follows further. To break the social law will win a ticket to the prison while successfully breaking laws of physics will end up with the Nobel prize. In both ways, laws are broken. In one form, a person is a criminal while the second one sounds like a hero. Specific laws are made up by definition and agreement. Others - by necessity. It is not that hard to break the social code. Rules are made to be improved, simplified or broken. Quite harder is to smash down physics which governs the reality. The question is how it would be possible to do it after all.

Physics is not a matter of agreement. Reality ignores people's opinions unless it is social. Social reality is about perceptions. In here everything may be constructed regardless it is based on facts or not. Such is a warning sign. The social reality is social what makes this realm like another dimension floating in the air. Everything would be considered to be true as long as it remains social. Knowledge would be constructed in the interaction with other fellow humans where opinions become equal to facts. An opinion in social reality is like a fact in the physical one. Both are on the complex fabric of understanding representing different dimensions. Such is, however, the best way to tax oneself. Why is it so?

Historically, some time ago religion had privatised world truth. Now, something different will poison the mind. Inquisition had done an exceptional job at maintaining divine justice. You do not need a thermometer to measure a degree of fanaticism. It was excellent at ignoring facts and conflicting with reality. In a religious sense, no facts were necessary to prove anything. Everything religious were considered to be true.

Religious = Truth

For those who opposed this, had a party of religious justice with the unhappy ending. For torture and punishment served for a public entertainment when flames had boiled the blood in heretic's veins. Fortunately, the civilisation evolved - it became history, but why is it mentioned? Religion and inquisition had the power to decide what is right without any discussions. Then to impose its order on people against their will. Faith and reality were like two separated islands. Not on the multidimensional fabric but one fighting another.

Knowledge of patterns allows to translate it from one field to another. The troubling issue comes when reality governed by physics converts entirely to another. Like in the first law of thermodynamics - energy travels from one system to another. In this context, energy is finite - just the form changes. Having this in mind, the type of truth may change as well - every part of multidimensional fabric has its metrics. It brings the standard to define the way of thinking. The religious way of thinking is nothing, but religious. Real and religious would have their points of disagreement.

When physics define transition of the energy, you can imagine if everything based on science and logic gets converted into a social reality which becomes the ultimate fundamental of truth. Smells like different privatisation of truth - a social one. Religious justice had led actions to fanatic outcomes. On the same tone, social justice warriors resemble the same breed under a different name. If everything true becomes social, then social justice warriors become the brand new inquisition.

Social = Truth

If such an environment delivers round squares or rectangular circles in a social manner, it would have no other way but to be right. This would be another brand of fanaticism where only one option is open for a go. Perhaps it is a menace for a healthy mind. Delusions designed socially may be neither cooperative, tolerant nor polite. Such is the potential outcome to tax the mind and create the confusion. And then the mind losses its value due to taxes gained through prejudice.

The delusion there is very likely. Everybody learns things, many falls in love with them, few can escape this temptation. However, learning contributes to progress. Any achievement is barely available without learning. You can learn the methods, theories, opinions, and facts. Although there are many distinctions of knowledge, let's focus on four of them to extract a number to cover up the central area.

First of all, let's consider the methods. They are particular procedures to achieve something. Everyone has methods and ways how to do things. Training and practice is a place where everyone can get them. Everyone craves for a sense of achievement. With a method, there is always the way. For example, if someone wishes to lose weight - there is the way. If someone wants to increase one's wealth by 15% - there is the way. If one wants to travel the world - there is the way. You need to find a working one. Methods are for everything, the central question, however, lies in their effectiveness. Having a method and having a working one is quite a distinction, but there is always the way. Everyone can learn methods.

Second of all, everyone can learn theories. In history, there is always an active attempt to design a theory that would explain the world in an elegant picture. Theory of relativity, string theory or theory of everything. What matters is the attempt to put complexities under the flag. Theories do explain things or exist for their own sake. Even you, now, could invent a theory on something to explain complexities in the world. It may work for maintaining focus in distraction. The downside - it may be wrong. The main disadvantage of theories is they are capable of being wrong what is the most straightforward way to delude yourself.

Thirdly, opinions are learnable as well. Everyone can learn how others see the world. If such thing is important - another question. However, you can learn how your friends think or see things. You can discover the entire diversity of opinions available in the market. It is not that opinions are right or wrong, but perhaps difference or popularity are metrics. They have tremendous representing powers of diversity - they are shades of reality. You learn opinions, but the question would be why anyone should do so. Entertainment and insight are good reasons for it.

Lastly, there are facts to be learnt. Facts have other metrics to be judged from. They are quite a solid foundation of knowledge.

Popularity is not the favourite metric for them. They are either correct or not - it cannot be two facts stating different things. It is hardly possible to keep two different facts on the same thing - only one of them is correct. Everybody can learn facts - elements of truth. Capitals of the world - factual. World demographics - factual. Events' records - factual. Many things are factual. So they are learnable. You learn facts and operate in facts. They give a significant sense of reality.

Judging by those four examples, you can learn quite a variety of things. Methods, theories, opinions, and facts - visible learnable elements. However, not all learning has a bright side. Learning may lead to the deception to perplex your mind to deliver complexity. Faulty things will bring you down due to the conflict. This is an unexpected divorce with reality. Poisonous knowledge will quickly cause one. Knowledge is empowering unless it has viruses.

Such errors tax and impair the mind. That is where the logic in quest is the remedy to automatic thinking.

The plot twist comes when learning goes unexpectedly unwell. You already know that the concept of the mental architecture represent logic and thinking patterns inside your head. Like a conventional one, it represents the specific property. The property has its taxes. Unfortunately, your mind also gets taxed for incoming knowledge settling there. So as the conventional property gets taxed, thus the mental one receives the very same treatment. Although, not in a monetary sense. Knowledge taxes the mind by turning it down.

There are sources to tax and turn your mind down - dysfunctional methods do not work, theories do not reflect reality, opinions are full of cats and facts are the beginning for the mental tax. Taxing effect is the reason for a massive delusion. Methods, theories, opinions, and facts are always open to question and inspection because believing in false leads to faulty. There is no use to keep up with unproductive deception. Productive deception at least gives practical result despite the mind being deceived. The question is always a missing element - which one. It varies among individuals.

The real problem appears when the holder mixes own perception and reality and so get into the conflict because they do not match together. That is the issue which may be happening in mind. Naturally, in the Age of Information, individuals get bombarded continuously with various sorts of information. It is the input. There is more and more information with less and less meaning. When this understanding does not match with the held awareness, then something goes wrong.

Although learning is intentionally beneficial, too much of it confuses the mind. Knowledge becomes a property of the mind, so it "needs to pay taxes." When the mentality is taxed, the potential is limited, and the performance may suffer. Mental taxes come in the form of distractions or overthinking along the way. Things around may be heavily distracting, especially in the Information Age.

Think of lenses looking through the world. Having the standard way of acting or thinking is common. Distinct societies have their ways to do things where the culture develops in people. For example, people who were raised to have particular religious beliefs they will perceive the world according to this mode of thinking. Things get looked through religious lenses. People who were raised in a highly materialistic society may worship material - things get looked though materialistic lenses. People raised in a socialistic society, so things are viewed through social lenses. Even the cultivation of culture will bring lenses to access things culturally. It is like a priority, picking one type of lenses do not let to see what others can show. All of the alternatives seem to be hanging on the complex fabric of understanding.

The problem is there are as many lenses as you want. However, some lenses see the reality distortedly different than it comes. Reality and perception may not match together as the glove matches the hand. It may cause issues. It is true that things you have done and things you have been exposed to form the way of thinking right now. It is one way of doing things compared to existing potential on multidimensional fabric. Much depends on the personal background. Education and learning bring enough influence to shape the direction of thinking. The problematic aspect is that someone becomes blind to what is unfamiliar.

Methods are the first mental tax to turn the mind down. First, it sounds counter-intuitive because methods are for solving problems. Not all methods are for every problem. As you remember functionality - methods are for a particular thing. Someone cannot just start diving with hot air balloon. Also, it is hardly productive to play music with a photo editor or edit photos with a music player. Methods do not work there. They were designed with the purpose in mind. Just because someone has the music player, one cannot edit photos despite the burning desire to do so. Or only because someone has the "right" key will not open up the chest because the key will not fit. The fitness is the standard for methods.

In this case, dysfunctional methods create a disturbing effect on the mind. It is sometimes quite common when methods worked in the past excellently suddenly stop showing its progressive value now. Especially when facing never seen problems. Repeating wise or professionally tied methods to something novel may not work. Then if methods do not work in solving problems, the chest cannot be cracked. Then the mind gets taxed by the unworkable method. Comfortable thinking may repeat the pattern expecting results while a new approach is on demand. Problems shall be solved, but methods do not do their job. It takes your energy and time but does not bring enough value.

Methods evolve along with problems. If methods stayed static, they would be incapable of cracking evolving problems. You will see that the application of futile methods ends up in vain. Methods work, but not for everything. Then some adjustments are needed. Complexity and problems rise, so the method should not lose the race. For a method to stay static, problems become superior. You know that products get their upgrade. Same said about software - it receives its update. This way they become better. Are there any methodical improvements to the mind? If not, the problem improves in complication until the unworkable method tax the mind impairing the confidence in abilities as well.

The second tax comes when theories are misleading. Theories are to explain general principles elegantly. This is the starting point to the conflict with reality. For example, the flat Earth theory distorts the perception of its holders. Surprisingly there is even a Flat Earth society to advocate that Earth is flat. Perhaps like a pizza. Those who hold beliefs about such theory will get into conflict not only with reality, but also with those who do not think this way. The answer to the conflict is to challenge by questioning it. Theories are grand unless they are misleading. Questions, critical thinking and facts are the judges for the sake of mind's health.

Among theories, there many of such kind. Religion and politics are topics often suggested avoiding to have friendly conversations. What matters here is that politics and religion, as well as other fields, have their theories. No matter what you will take as a general entity - you will find theories. Economy, technology or science - you will find many to explain distinct things. They are helpful or misleading. The purpose is to reduce mental taxes, so probably those theories matching with reality like a glove matches the hand should get the favour - others are taxing.

To learn misleading theories will tax the mind because it creates a delusion. Once it faces the real world, it may bring the mind into confusion. That is the point where two opposite theories create the conflict. When the mind follows anything taxing, that is the beginning for something more intense. And then, instead of explaining the complexities elegantly, theories do something unexpected. Theories designed to simplify things, increase complexity instead. They misexplain and therefore bring more complexity than they reduce. That is the tax which slows down the mind and invites overthinking for a cup of tea. People believe in wrong things, but why should not they? Unfitting theories are worse than no theories at all.

The third way of taxing your mind comes in the form of opinions. Everybody has a view. If someone does not have it, one must check the pulse. Opinions are one of the most common forms of perception. The dangerous side, however, is that anyone gets themselves to become highly opinionated. Learning opinions for real would sound bizarre in the first place. As if collecting them like geological specimens. It may enrich view but at the same time inspires misconceptions.

Opinions are never right only different. They do not solve anything but bring some colours to the table. Being opinionated is not helpful in solving problems. Being submerged under the sea of opinions threatens to originality as someone may stop thinking and will only repeat words of others. Probably the most peaceful slavery is to follow opinions and to have none. So the question of learning them is not the case. Knowledge liberates, view delivers the shade of reality.

Getting your mind subjugated by opinions is a distinctively high tax to pay. It is not you who pays. It is not your mind which makes a transaction. However, your mind is what suffers. In becoming more and more opinionated and losing track of reality, someone may miss the line separating opinion and a fact. And when opinion mismatches reality, it could become like prejudice.

Imagine the situation. Someone shares its view which gets viral and therefore gets established for the face value. Someone influential may hold an opinion and make it public that crêpes with Nutella - called Nutellians - were the first civilisation to colonise the Moon. People will find it entertaining. It sounds sweet. It is not true but if accepted as such the mind gets taxed. Sometimes it is more dangerous than fun. It could outgrow into a fanatic religion. Just think - Nutellians.

As probably naturally inferred, opinions do not solve anything. They bring diversity which is excellent insight providers. They are about variety, not about truth. Surely, if someone has made no opinion by oneself, it will quickly make one distracted. Resembling the situation where winds play with a small ship in the ocean -

opinions are like winds. The taxing distraction gets through opinion - through many of them.

There is a fine line to border facts from fiction. Facts are an excellent motive for fiction that is why there are so many great books. Moreover, they are the source to twist perception and create something new. The sense of reality relies on them. Facts institute what is true where the world opens the gates for interpretations. Facts are objective and neutral. If they are different, only one is right.

The fastest way to become ridiculously biased is to collect opinions like berries and ignore facts. However, gathering facts are more useful berries; opinions have a better taste. It is not opinion what contributes to knowledge, but facts that build it. The view only reflects knowledge by giving various shades of it. Facts have their potential for the threat. Facts tax the mind in two ways. One comes from abundance, another in falsity.

Facts tax the mind in their abundance. In the rapid circulation of information, many things are going around. The mind is bombarded from all four directions. Information is everywhere, so the mind needs to deal with it. The disturbing part comes when the mind gets distracted by anything. The Information Age promises the vast circulation of facts around. The focus may be lost quickly. The loss of concentration - the taxing effect. Significant information or not - that is not the issue. All thinkable things turn the tax up because thoughts require a true treatment. The abundance of facts taxes the mind for it has to proceed such amount.

Secondly, facts could be a complete fabrication. Like someone bakes cakes, others bake fake fact cakes. Fiction could become a fact without anyone realising it. That could happen if all minds collectively accept what is real while reality has something to conceal. Media agencies providing fake news will serve for a notorious example. Such facts are fabricated to misinform. Then such facts tax the mind unless you question them.

So far so good. Learning has two sides of itself. You know its positive side intuitively. Learning accelerates accomplishments on the one hand. On the other hand, learning certain things tax the mind, so it loses its swiftness, effectiveness, and lightness. Then the mind perfectly represents a warehouse full of random elements to be used. Not the abundance that creates the challenge, but conflicting aspects of specific knowledge. The standard to separate this is quite straightforward. What neither bring value nor stand for neutrality, the chance is that this knowledge is toxic. Knowledge shall serve and encourage the mind without being wasteful to slow it down.

Coming back to methods - methods are designed to work, so unfitting methods tax the performance of the mind. Just think when theories misrepresent the reality - someone holding prejudice may see no conflict, but it brings a person in denial once it faces reality. Just think about when the abundance of opinions enters the scene. The tax comes when the wealth of opinions lullabies judgement. Just think about when alternative facts replace the natural perception of reality - this is fabricated. Alternative facts or fake news - both are misleading. The mind that accepts this for real when reality has something to conceal - taxed.

Hopefully, standards dictate the priorities of the incoming. People do not listen to everyone. The way to approach the situation is to think. To think means to question, so starting with a question turns on more critical approach rather than an obedient stand. Otherwise, things tax the mind, so it goes like additional and harmful luggage. Something to be prevented by asking questions to approach things in their light. Critical thinking and the logic in quest are the medicine to reduce the taxing effect on the mind.

Eventually, when the mind becomes taxed excessively, it outgrows into the cognitive entanglement. The state is entirely psychological. The perplexity of mind is coming from complexity of things. The obvious misunderstanding, misconception, and the total loss. The issue is not with the reality but with the perception of it. That is the tornado of complexity penetrating the mind. Mental taxes make the mind unproductive for its value get drained for nothing. In this way, the mind is more likely to be useless. That is where the person, if caught in this situation, shall start managing complexity by following the leadership of questions. Follow complexity or your questions - something to choose.

The cognitive entanglement looks like activity with no action. Someone analyses things til they paralyse. Does not sound very mobile. Thinking is invisible unless it reveals in practice. The cognitive entanglement puts the mind into the quicksand. It is very simple. When the mind does not manage complexity, then complexity manages the mind. The mind loses its independent powers. Then problems become vague, and hesitation comes in decisions. There, knowledge gained through learning may be the bless and curse. It enriches the perspective of the world, but at the same time, it can debilitate an individual mind by making it fragmented and lost.

It is not enough to think, actions are essential. The cognitive entanglement - it deflects efforts where actions do not happen. The cognitive entanglement is the confusion and noise in mind as rapid and continually going as tweets. Tweets in your dashboard are manageable. The mind is too. Learning is not always as productive as you have seen. Learning false things cripples the mind and populates it with prejudice. Mental tax reduces the value of mind it produces. From the cognitive entanglement and perplexing thoughts - the question is the way out. That is the way to think out. The question is the answer to navigate this.

Eventually, entangling consequences may bring hard times for decisions to be made and problem solving faculty in general. The mind becomes more consuming and wasteful than productive. Then is the time when either mind solves itself or problems around solve it. It is not only the hardship coming from overthinking, but also problems will hinder your mind. So the mind shall wake up and manage the flow to stand up against the incoming pressure. The mind shall manage complexity and solve problems before it happens the other way round. The question is the answer.

Finally, learning may be pumping poisonous understanding to your mind. So the mind shall have its immune system from viruses and issue thinking policies to reduce taxes. As you are familiar, knowledge represents mental property. Mental taxes charge a fee for the mind's potential. Inevitably you ask questions and think out to solve problems and untangle complexities. And the medicine for entanglement there the step of detachment. As the name speaks for itself - the act to dissect unnecessary elements from the mind to operate fully. The question would be how to detach from what is familiar and comfortable to make the mind finer.

The Step of Detachment

"The difficulty lies not so much in developing new ideas as in escaping from old ones."
John Maynard Keynes

Prejudice, wishful thinking, and denial are not obvious in the first place. But if the person is cognitively entangled, the reason goes on vacation. So precision of logic and clarity of intellect do not attend the party. Obedient thinking acts obediently. Then, the mind obeys to complexity like falling bricks respect the laws of physics. Not the best way to solve trouble because the mind is in a self-created bubble. To avoid confusion, one needs to make some exclusion. Less property - fewer taxes. Even though the currency is not monetary, it receives tax what put the mind into its traps. What matters is how you think, not which thoughts have shown their ink. A mode beats the load. That is why detachment from common knowledge is the starting point for the mind to wake up.

You remember that learning is electricity of progress. Equally, it may lead to the cognitive entanglement. Any attempt to connect progress and entanglement into a single entity may end up in contradiction. Progress and entanglement - two potential ends. Progress sometimes is complicated where management of it brings positive results. On the one hand, progress gets its support from conclusions and consequences. Output comes from active or pensive work. Then, learning increases productivity and productive work leads to improvement. On the other hand, learning may evolve into the cognitive entanglement where the mind taxes itself excessively to end up standing in the quicksand. The mind moves around without a clear purpose for if it had a purpose, it would move towards it. An immobile thing does not change, improve or progress. The cognitive entanglement is frozen in a vicious circle; progress is moving straightforwardly.

You have discovered that learning of misleading things shapes a convicted mind. The conviction which resembles prejudice does not inspire for quality decisions. The mind gets in denial. Especially in thinking, prejudice is the tax to refrain from actions. Denial will be unproductive. Just imagine an astrophysicist believing in flat Earth theory refusing facts standing against that. What would be the scientific output of this? Or imagine a geologist thinking that earth of age would be only 6000 years. The geologic time scale would be a real challenge for scientific work. Also, museum collections would look like a practical joke for such mind. People are free to believe in anything. The point is made - it disables the mind. The mind is a priceless organisation, but some sell it to unpaid servitude without a second thought.

Problems like decisions are the central topic. It is rare to solve things you do not understand. Seeing a problem is the part of the solution. However, if the mind gets taxed or infected, so problems become vague. If someone finds a solution without having a problem - curiously enough - what is the problem the solution tried to solve? The grip of the problem is a reason for the solution. If the mind cannot see the problem - the solution does not come. The cognitive entanglement brings its complexity to impair the vision of this kind.

When people accept anything for real when reality had something to conceal it leads to certain blindness. The mind gets misguided and does not see the problem. Complexity could be the serious hinder - even brilliant minds get blinded at times. Learning things may bring confusing elements. Questions are the agent for the mind to wake up. Indoctrination is misguided learning that mismatch with reality. To find out weak spots of problems - target them with questions. If you do not like questions - think. To think is to question and to question is to think.

Let's start again going with the striking analogy. Many times you will find similarities between people's way of thinking and that of a computer. Humans have a similar logic as a computer does. Too much information slows down not only computers, but people's mind too - people get overwhelmed. There is the taxing element. Computers proceed files, humans - memories, thoughts, emotions, etc. Also, like computers, the person can experience a mental breakdown if one is overwhelmed. The computer starts working slower and lags because of bugs, trash and infected files coming into the system. Like human mind, you already discovered similar potential - random input, misguided learning and mental viruses tax the mind. Does not sound helpful to solve problems. That is where detachment from the irrelevant is part of the solution.

For comparison, new computers function significantly greater than old ones. Following this analogy, the mind is similar. The thing to realise is to understand that the way you think logically is similar to a computer program. Computers run on programs; the mental architecture is the code where thought is set in the cultivated order. The attitude there talks for itself. Clean and unaffected computer system works substantially faster than one with problems. Equally, the clearer mind is faster compared to baffled and overcomplicated one. This is where detachment from the taxing elements improves the mind. That is where the detachment cleans the clutter.

Moreover, in computer science, the algorithm is superior to information where the algorithm governs it. You will call it a habit of the computer. In other words, the algorithm is the government for information as well as the mental architecture is the government of individual knowledge. However, they become pointless if there is no information to govern. The analogy is designed to fit humans. Like a computer, the human mind runs on a specific function - the mindset. That is the program in mind. When the algorithm governs information, the mindset governs your universe.

Programs, as well as mindsets, work with particular things they were initially designed. Music player plays music, and photo editor edits photos. Look at reverse. If you need to edit photos - you buy a photo editing program, if listening to the music is on demand, you buy a music player. The functionality here is quite fixed. Can you imagine a person who edits photos with the music player, or listens to the music with a photo editor? Something would not work. Neither music will get played nor pictures edited. This is the analogy to your mind if it applies unfitting mindsets.

Equally, the mindset gets developed to fit for a particular task. Someone is good at people, some excellent with numbers, others work well with words or pictures. Variety of applications possible is indeed staggering. No matter which mindset you would decide to pick up. All of them have the mental architecture behind which, by the way, is weightless. The mindset stands there for its function. For an individual, it is rare to solve problems if the mindset is not designed for the challenge. As if opening the chest with the unfitting key - it does not open. Your mind is the problem solver - the key to crack chests.

This is the place which is telling that new problem will require fresh intelligence to solve them. So then people learn and upgrade their potential to solve problems. The mind is liquid and functional. If the problem is analytic, the mind readjusts to solve it. If the problem is conceptual, the mind regroups to solve it. If the problem is organisational, the mind adapts to solve it. If the problem is technical, the mind changes to solve it. The mind is like a function;

it matches the problem to solve it. It forges the fitting key for the chest to get opened.

The mental architecture in people is surprising in diversity. No matter the initial state, existing knowledge may be the barrier keeping you from moving forward. Knowledge will be heavy to carry. For the problem not all known things are relevant. A certain type of knowledge, as well as the mindset, does not fit as a key to open up the chest.

Being irrelevant they only take precious place in mind. Just think what use will be for a pilot to know species of scorpions or for a miner to recognise bird flocks. Such are random examples to represent two sets of knowledge. It shows the person is knowledgeable about what is not relevant to what they do. A knowledgeable person is knowledgeable, but the problem solver solves problems. You decide which one is smarter - one who carries knowledge or who applies it.

Learning is one thing, jumping among learnings is another. It should not look like another term to stand for distraction. When the keen mind sees the complex fabric of understanding, all knowledge possible has the uniting logic behind which eyes cannot see. If the mind is light enough, it can transcend from one set of knowledge to another without penalties to solve problems. The mind adjusts a type of knowledge according to the type of a problem. The mind itself is a light function. Knowledge gets value in action and declines in possession - that is what one shall keep in mind with any learning opportunity.

What is helpful is the detachment. The forceful act of knowledge suspension to start from basics without cognitive penalty. Going back to the principles is the starting point to avoid complexity in mind and solve problems instead of falling into them. Walking away from the problem suspends your potentially emotional response. Solving problems is not the act of emotions because sentiments bring additional weight without solving anything. The person gets attached to the problem then. The problem becomes like furniture - you do not want to throw it out. Or like a garden - you do not want to abandon it. The solution is the death of a particular problem, so exchanging a problem into a solution is the loss. Therefore, in this context, losing problems means victory.

But before, the step of detachment removes the perplexity. To solve the problem of self-delusion is to challenge and eliminate your thoughts. In other words, to make the mind lightweight for receiving lower cognitive tax. People will quickly fall into wishful thinking or be overthinking. Far from being exciting boosters. That is why detachment removes the unnecessary weight.

Lower taxes, more profit. The cognitive entanglement starts disentangling itself once there is no material to chain the mind and cause attitude problems. Thinking patterns are more important than thinkable things. Intelligence is superior to knowledge.

Everyone can collect data; thinking methods are developed. Methods flex problems into solutions while data show things, but never solve or decide anything. A particular method is the function of mind to advance knowledge somewhere because knowledge alone has no motivation to go anywhere.

The question is a light and elegant start for everything. The leadership of it is the natural act to delegate your mind to resolve the trouble. If overthinking would be a type of government, it would be the wealthiest agency in the universe for collecting such taxes. So detachment from abundant and unnecessary knowledge is the step to make. It is a smart way to solve the problem before it solves the solver. Problems will be your master which may cause you a beautiful disaster. That is why you solve them before they complicate things and solve you. So the mind detaches from mental property.

Falling in love with ideas is a romantic act. Falling out of love with them is a rational adventure. To detach from concepts, experiences and emotions is the natural way to face the music. The step of detachment is falling out of personal perspective to end idealistic flirtation and wake up. Having ideas is luxury while thinking is more expensive. However, to solve the problem, knowledge is priceless, irrelevant knowledge is taxing. Detachment releases the excess. The logic in quest challenges mental property. To keep or sweep it off.

Forget what you have learnt intentionally - is the ultimate maxim. The step of detachment is a temporary suspension from automatic thinking. So you are a knowledgeable person. Forget what you know to approach things from basics. The replacement of learning into thinking is the fragile change because learning is comfortable compared to thinking. Isaac Newton, once in Cambridge, was suspended from studies like all students due to plague in 1665. Studies and learning the lore was replaced with thinking in the end. Newton thought out, so he invented calculus, discovered Laws of Motion and force of gravity. Newton could not learn this, so he thought out. Your mind equally needs to start thinking instead of collecting knowledge like archaeological artefacts.

It is the destiny of fool to be educated only by the public school. Knowledge is imperfect. Thinking solves problems where learning collects solutions. Learning is oxygen for thought where burning reaction happen. But learning should not be the ultimate performance. Learning makes you a learner where the failure of applying knowledge promises an unproductive existence. Learning gives you coloured glasses with more lenses, but it is you who needs to take a look through them.

To speak amusingly, problems are capricious - they demand specific solutions. You need to craft them from learning. The mind shall see more than from one perspective, and sometimes to do so, one needs to learn profoundly but abandon it to start thinking from basics again. Intelligence uses knowledge to solve problems. More people can be proud of knowledge they have - fewer with intelligence. Everyone can get knowledge by holding one's attention for three seconds to gather it. Intelligence may require more than three seconds.

Then for the mind to be useful and insightful, it needs to learn how to see. When both eyes are occupied with incapable lenses, the view does not show anything new. The act is to find the solution. If it is invisible, perhaps incorrect lenses are in use. You cannot observe the behaviour of molecules with the telescope. Lenses are unfit. If someone used a microscope for observing planets - unsuitable lenses would take your time in vain. Lenses allow approaching reality. Like your attitude which shows and makes up your mind. However, learning how to see it is an expensive investment because it does not turn into reward immediately. One needs to learn how to see. Otherwise, someone will look at molecules with a telescope and would see nothing. To solve a problem and see the solution, the right lenses shall turn down fences.

Learning and thinking are those powers which write down a symphony. Learning gives information while thinking applies its logic. Unlearning makes thinking lighter. Time is limited - learning means learning, thinking means thinking. With that being said, being occupied with learning leaves less time to think. But as you know, the stomach cannot work without food as well as the mind cannot operate without experience. Learning is essential, but the time you detach from the material, it has more space and time for creative manoeuvring.

That is where the step of detachment is the falling out of love with ideas. The mind stops flirtation with the familiar. It sounds like the divorce with your comfortable state of mind. Do not get it wrong. Knowledge is substantially effective. But if it contradicts with existing preconceptions, it will tax your mind and impair its performance. If it does, it shall detach from both contradicting sides and look at the basic principles. To unlearn things is like throwing out luxurious furniture or abandoning a lovely garden. A complete suspension of knowledge reduces the impact of biases.

Moreover, the step of detachment removes cosmetics from the problem. It disengages with familiar luggage and enters a new field. Then every problem shows its identity in the natural light. Although problems do not have a passport, questions redesign their identity to figure out an elegant solution. A failure to understand the character of a problem retains it. To put simply, worries, overthinking and the emotional train put cosmetics on everything, so the problem remains covered, vague or invisible. Cosmetics does not solve problems but make them look agreeable and nice-looking. That is why to solve a problem there is the need to remove cosmetics. The step of detachment goes towards that direction.

Good looking things are naturally inviting. Cosmetics will cover up and stimulate the mind but hardly dissect the problem. Even though learning enriches the perspective, cosmetics cover up issues. The cognitive entanglement is the source for all problems in mind. One needs to wake up. Problems hide its real face if it is covered with cosmetics. It is delusional. In this case, straight questions decolour and expose it.

So instead of letting problems to integrate into the natural fibre of the mind, it divorces with knowledge by suspension. Intuitively, learning leads to understanding. Then, building up knowledge out of misleading things entangle your mind accordingly. The step of detachment achieves the objectivity needed for the complex problem to get defeated. Detachment from knowledge makes your attitude naked. A vulnerable moment to extract the intelligent function led by the logic in quest. Then the problem exposes its identity. Cosmetics fades away, so you take into a direct solving action.

Suspending judgement is the way of going light. Less is more. If thoughts have weight, then developed ideas have more weight. However, it is not weight measured by SI units. It is cognitive luggage that weights. Enlarging the field of vision releases the performance where everything connects to everything. And to get more space means to detach from what occupies it. Detachment implies conversion into the going light state. In other words, the walk away from what is familiar. Thinking expedites solutions to problems, so it is precious to have the mind sharp, swift and lively rather than bulky, slow and full of everything.

Moving forward. To think is to compute. Light is not the mode of disability. Just compare two devices: ENIAC (electronic numerical integrator and computer) and modern day smartphone. ENI-

AC was one of the earliest computers which was unusually heavy and large. It was 1800 square meters big and 30 tons heavy. Just imagine carrying such in a pocket.

A modern-day smartphone would not cause much discomfort. Processes got refined, and the design improved, so many carries 175 grams device in the pocket having even more computing power. 175 grams are slightly lighter than 30 tons. Such an example illustrates the mind perfectly. Would you prefer a bulky or light one? Going light resembles refinement. Improved computers work faster and require less space. Just wonder what would happen with a mental upgrade by detaching from the redundant? To compute is to think.

So it is about detaching from complexity of information and start going in the light mode. It is quite obvious, is not it? Cognitive luggage has its disadvantages. If you take traveling, you will discover a clear difference. To move a long distance with a single backpack is more comfortable and lighter than carrying three gigantic suitcases. Remember, that you have two hands. It is a matter of question what is inside, but even the most expensive property reduces the speed. Speed is what separates entangled mind and lightweight one - going light speeds up the mind accordingly. Life is like a journey nonetheless - moving faster brings one further with the logic in quest.

For the mind to reduce the taxing effect, the ingenious solution is to own only little and the most essential property. Everything you need will be accessible. Keeping the mind as a function to be applied rather than a property to be held. That is to say about knowledge - knowledge in use is superior to knowledge in possession. You know that multiplicity of things in your head will cause potential overthinking which solves nothing. The less mental property, the fewer taxes. Eventually, the lighter the mind, the better it functions. The aim is to keep the mind light.

To think swiftly, the mind must be lightweight. Overthinking is not the cool thing to be proud of. Everybody can get knowledgeable. The better question is how to apply knowledge productively. Every fool can learn and bring random stuff into one's head. Way more clever would be to preselect the most fitting pieces and use them. The secret lies in putting the function of knowledge on priority and keeping knowledge secondary. Learning is active, but knowledge is static. Thinking mobilises knowledge - thinkable things get in action what could derive novelty.

It is not necessary to travel a long distance to redress the attitude. The act of changing is like putting new clothes on. In this case, it is undressing from knowledge and start from basics again towards complexity. For those wondering how the step of detachment solves problems, the answer comes like this. The disconnection put a problem farther from your mind to see it better - in distance. Having this relationship - it does not tax the mind, so it starts the polite violence against problems. The step of detachment leads into the state of going light.

Going Light

> *"Instead of cursing the darkness, light a candle."*
> **Benjamin Franklin**

Going light is the result of detachment. This part relies on the function which has no weight. If it does - so how much it weights then? Skills are of this kind. The mental architecture has no weight as well as triadic style, so the logic in quest weights the same. Thinking patterns tend to be weightless. For the step of detachment is to see the pattern. The pattern of thinking where the light way excludes everything to see what is left. When everything is eliminated, the pattern remains - this is the intelligent function and the logic in quest to use in the compass.

First, think about how much reading skills weight. Books and written papers have their weight expressions. Reading skills are applied like a weightless function. To read and something to be read - a difference. One is visible; another is invisible. Two realities where the skin is the line of separation. One world around the surface and another one under it. Such is the distinction between physical and mental. Although the physical objects around the skin have weight, the mental function is lightweight.

Second, think about how much driving skills weight. Cars and motorcycles have their weight expressions. Driving skills are applied like a weightless function. To drive and something to be driven - a distinction. Two realities where the skin is the line of separation. One world around the surface and another one under it. Such is the difference between physical and mental. Although the physical objects around the skin have weight, the mental function is lightweight.

Lastly, think about how much numeric skills weight. Plates, books or cars have their weight expressions. Digital skills are applied like a weightless function. To count or something to be counted - a gap. Two realities where the skin is the line of separation. One world around the surface and another one under it. Such is the distinction between physical and mental. Although the physical objects around the skin have weight, the mental function is lightweight.

The state of going light reduces the cognitive luggage promisingly. A weightless end is the most radical outcome of detachment. The truth is, forgetting everything what you learnt is a challenging task. More clever is to suspend knowledge before tackling the problem and putting a clean slate for incoming decisions. Such is a non-taxing way to approach anything new. Then held preconceptions do not interrupt into a new campaign, so the mind is less likely to be entangled. For problem solving and decision making, the light way is less taxing.

The concept of going light is weightless. Moreover, going light is an athletic mode for problems. The mind is sharper when it is lighter. As well as athletes are faster in sprint or marathon if they are lean and well trained. Olympian athletes or athletic minds - both are running. Running a sprint or a marathon is like solving problems. Equally, problems have their mixed distances - some are urgent while others not. Some are simple, and others are heavier. They take time like sprints or marathons before you can finish one or another. The metaphor of going light is the detachment from things what makes your mind heavy, slower or confused. Going light is preventing you from mental obesity.

Beside many skills, your mental architecture is a weightless function as well. Thinking logically is the flair like any others. It inspects information and deduces conclusions based on its laws -

the rules of the game. Abstract or critical thinking activate inspecting of what is given. Logic does not create anything, but works with what is presented. The mental architecture in general is the skeleton and structure to be applied. It has its laws of logic to use without a pause.

Moreover, triadic style is weightless in the same way. Triadic style is the skill as any others. It functions on grammar which gets its life through logic. It extends logical limitations to go abroad the logical island. Verbal aspect is a different island to bring fitness and produce questions. For it to function your mental architecture is the foundation. Triadic style is like muscles flexing up for making questions. This is the attitude which goes inside out. From the basic principles, the expansion sets the direction outwards.

The logic in quest is the skeleton and muscles combined. Logic alone is like a skeleton. Questions are mobilising muscles. Naturally, muscles are placed on the skeleton as well as you build up questions on grammar. So the logic in quest is the skeletal muscle to employ intelligence to solve problems and make decisions.

Then there is a finalising piece - a complex fabric of understanding. Speaking metaphorically, multifaceted thinking resembles dressing up the mind. You have discovered that there is a broad world of cultures, backgrounds, special knowledge, etc. The mind will dress up itself with one of those to see the world from various perspectives. Dressing up the mind with special knowledge allows viewing the world through the lenses they provide to manage complexity.

In the end, you aware that the tree of knowledge has many branches. As if all of them lie down on the complex fabric. The mind will get taxed from the excessive learning if no application gets real. To learn false things for your mind will cause the entanglement. This is the time where detachment and going light are aligning your mind. As already mentioned - new problems are capricious. They demand uniquely tailored solutions. Going light is the mode for crafting them by gathering intelligence lightly even if knowledge is heavy itself. The step of detachment separates entanglement and the mind like two islands.

This is for complexity management. Complexity gets managed when the noise does not hide like in Brazilian jungles, but gets naked like in the African desert. Complexity is tackled directly without entanglements then. When the mind dissects from the limiting luggage, then it wakes up and sees things in their light. Eventually, the mind is no longer covered with pieces of knowledge imaginable which grows a jungle in your mind to hide complexity. When things get on the surface on the desert - there is no place for complexity to hide. Then the mind sees its enemy for piercing, deconstructing or refining it.

When the mind is light, there is more space for creative manoeuvring to tackle problems and make decisions without hard feelings. The mind would act like the engine which solves problems according to the patterns and makes decisions according to standards. No complexity can match such mind without evolving. When complexity increases, the mind extends as well to bring it down. A constant competition what brings progress in the end.

When the mind becomes light one, it leaves enough space for the intelligence to have fun. When the mind is complicated with unimportant things, it demobilises itself. Keeping the mind light leaves space for spontaneity to fuel creativity and tackle the mind's obesity. The fourth principle of questology makes the mind lightweight for liberating oneself from the self-imposed limits to act swiftly against what is inevitable - complexity.

A lighter mind has more life because it does not carry entangling knowledge. A human mind is not a computer system, but may act like one. For making decisions and solving problems, thinking and computation may be the mode of action. Questions navigate thinking and computing. Questions lead the mind while you govern this leader. Then problems meet their solution to end the confusion. Also, decisions become based not on air but instead on the proficient flair. All patterns and all standards are questionable as well as they are acceptable. For building something greater, the start will bring a result later. The question is the answer when a frozen mind converts into a dancer.

Questology

THE ENDING NOTE

Now, you have a compass at the moment which is a beautiful component. Of the mind to navigate with the logic in quest to find answers you need. The compass of the mind is the expansive thinking to expand the comfort. Even though this compass is invisible, through four principles, you approached practical utility to operate with agility.

The first principle instituted a logical link where the question ends up with the answer. This would undoubtedly keep aspirations stable because every question connects with the answer. Like the ship leaving Rotterdam approaches London or the signal gets broadcast and received. The bond is invisible where it stands at place for certainty. For someone who doubts, the bond is the link to follow. Questions lead to answers. Then if you need answers, you start asking your questions with the logic in quest.

The bond is ideally appearing to display the relationship between the present and the future. You wonder and question things now, but answers come in the future. Questions become a way where you convert future into the present by pushing present to the future. Questology serves for guidance where question connects to answers. Then there is hope in numbers to learn the future which had never happened so, therefore, learnt in a different way than the past is. Learning the future has another aspect.

To exercise the vision of the future eventually converts future into presence - then it comes learnable to everyone. The first principle touched the concept of time where two options are present. First one flows with the time realistically while another one jumps mentally forward into seeing the future sooner than it presents itself. Close or distant future is future after all. So putting future into present faster than it comes naturally makes it learnable sooner.

The second principle extended the link till the full scope of the mental architecture. As you have realised, such is invisible, inaudible and untouchable like many smart things are. The mental architecture is the structure and logic which often defines what makes sense or not. The clear scope of utility where it institutes the foundation for logical thinking to approach things critically in the most neutral light. Zooming things like a microscope, deconstructing them like a hammer or removing them out like a shaver. Faculties of the mind undoubtedly contribute to tackling the main two things this book is aimed at. The mental architecture is the secret government which is like the intelligent function in the brain.

First of all, information is vital to making decisions. The Information Age will offer a vast circulation of it. With great information comes great responsibility and struggle. Your mind could get lost quickly unless it employs standards of behaving with it. The mental architecture sets up standards to behave with information to use it for greater good. The standard is the justice for decision making. Designed for the benefit while remaining questionable.

Secondly, problems may come in various shapes. The mental architecture is the patterned ability to solve them with agility. To solve problems, mind evolves faster than the problem does. Otherwise, it stays at risk of being overwhelmed. Patterns build up the ground. Things are open to being pierced, deconstructed or refined - plain acts to perform a polite hostility against complexity barriers between you and future. Complexity is pierced, deconstructed, refined, and, eventually tamed to make it manageable. The mental architecture behaves with raw complexity to design a refined composition according to its picture.

Thirdly, the mental architecture is the foundation for the logic in quest. Logic alone is the immobile skeleton. To make it practical and useful, one gets in motion. Logic does not do anything constructive, but pierce everything critically and autocratically. What is wrong does not live for long. Wrong facts, theories, and conclusions die - useless to apply in spite of their unlimited supply. To progress, logic gets its extension for the logic in quest. The question is the addition.

The logic in quest is the third principle of the compass you have discovered. Any question stands on grammar where it relies on logic. So there your mental architecture becomes the foundation for the question. Then the logic in quest operates lightly with the intentions built on it. Logic combined with preferences of your personality guides you towards the direction silently shouted in your mind. Partly, the logic in quest goes for definition, explanation, and reason.

It is enough to see that in the complex world of overstimulation of information everyone will become easily distracted without putting boundaries on complexity. You know that defined things are easier to understand. In solving problems and making decisions, clarity is the way to go. Unclear, even invisible problems or dilemmas may cause a taxing effect. It sounds intuitive when you see problems or dilemmas; you can tackle them. Partial invisibility is just taxing without any profit. That is why definitions gained through the logic in quest are valuable.

Moreover, knowing how things work bring additional confidence in decisions. Explanation questions were to penetrate more in-depth than the surface of the definition. They aim to explain unclear things. Understanding how things work is the beginning of creating useful things. The start for innovation and invention are beneath the surface. There is always the mechanism beneath the facade. Defining the watch does not explain how it works. The explanation is the extension.

Where the logic in quest strikes, you often do not ignore reason. There are two types of which you have realised. One goes for the inspirational source that something in the future pulls you to explain why you do what you do. Another subtle aspect stands for causality which detects reasons for problems. Then questions are guiding to solve the cause. Questions of reason target both future and the present by uniquely approaching them.

The logic in quest is piercing things up. For better-defined targets, askability score ranks them up. It is relatively painless to question things with the flair. Coming with the power of structure it is not enough to back questions on slim intention. Questions shall be relevant. Slightly defined by interest, context, and impact they have on existing conditions. Askability score is a judge to maintain the standard and focus on where the mind shall be pointing at. The fitness of the question consists of active efforts to exercise your mind in triadic style according to or against askability score.

The final fourth principle is about complexity management. To solve problems and make decisions, intelligence is of value. Learning is building up the complex understanding which is valuable for managing complexity before it controls you. For thoughts and actions, confidence comes from learning. It boosts real intelligence, so the person will go forward to employ knowledge. Learning is electricity to charge intentions to convert them into actions. Ignorance is not the tiger to make the fire. Learning is electricity for developing an ability.

When it comes to the complex world, regarding learning, to squeeze an expert, it is enough to integrate the set of knowledge into a person. There are many walks of life. To make someone a lawyer, one needs a person and law training. To make someone a medic, it needs a person and medical training. To make someone a scientist, it needs a person and scientific training. In this case, the equation is straightforward, knowledge forms a person as the representative of specific knowledge. This suggests a vast and complicated diversity. So to understand and manage complexity, it is beneficial to see the world holistically - as if things were lying down on the complex fabric of understanding.

Learning makes a person more ready to apply knowledge. Knowledge and information are essential for solving complex problems and making quality decisions. Curse of knowledge may come in many forms. You realised that learning could cause the mind to malfunction what is not a desired thing. Elements in mind form mental property getting taxes to turn the mind down. Slowing effect is negative as well as entanglement what keeps the mind in confusion.

To remove prejudice, devastating taxes, and mental viruses - the step of detachment will show its muscles. It detaches and suspends from knowledge and enters the light state. When the mind is not pressed by limiting or cursing learning, then it goes light to solve problems and make decisions. This is a swift glide through the book.

To the final note - this is the blueprint for the mind after all. Complexities are too complicated to reveal them simply. Having a compass and the framework serves as the first design to approach problems, decisions and command yourself forward. Future is in the perspective where past becomes effective. Current problems and whatemmas are stopping someone from going there. The light mode goes with the compass of the mind. Questology is the rational design to form questions towards the intended direction.

Four principles connect questions with answers, then form a personal government, goes with the logic in quest through the complex world. The world is complex, so having one perspective is not always helpful to grasp the scope. The compass of the mind does not leave anyone behind. Problems get unlocked, decisions become firm where the leadership of the question is using the compass with the logic in quest. Things change if you move. Questions are more important than answers, but you need answers. Therefore, you start with your questions because your mind is no longer the mind, but the compass - use it.

www.ingramcontent.com/pod-product-compliance
Lightning Source LLC
Chambersburg PA
CBHW071612220526
45469CB00002B/326